STORI[illegible] M THE GENBA

CONVERSATIONS WITH JAPAN-INSIDER COUNTRY MANAGERS

FRANK FOLEY & DAVID PINSKER

Next Big
Thing Co., Ltd.

Stories From The Genba: Conversations With
Japan-Insider Country Managers
By Frank Foley & David Pinsker

Published by Next Big Thing Co., Ltd.
937-196 Tokiwa, Kamakura, Kanagawa, Japan

contact_us@countrymanagers.jp
www.linkedin.com/in/frankfoleyjapan

Cover design Brian Smith (www.designmanjapan.com)

ISBN 978-4-9913127-2-4 (softcover)
ISBN 978-4-9913127-1-7 (ebook)

Next Big
Thing Co., Ltd.

AUTHOR PROFILES

Frank Foley has lived and worked in Japan for 33 years, including 22 years as Country Manager for family-oriented consumer goods and entertainment properties. He has managed major foreign brands including Thomas and Friends, National Geographic Channel, Guinness World Records, and HarperCollins Publishers. He has extensive experience in business development, and brand and character licensing across a range of industry sectors. Frank is currently serving as the Japan Country Manager for The East India Company Ltd.

David Pinsker has worked with Italian and German-owned companies in dealing with Japan. He was the first Japan-resident manager at De Agostini, where he was involved in establishing its organizational structure and in negotiations with Japanese business partners and distributors. More recently he headed up corporate communications in Japan for the German materials and bio-pharma company Merck. He has also held positions at the world-renowned Nature Magazine, the art publisher Taschen, the computer game maker Infogrames, and the German Chamber of Commerce in Japan. He is an independent consultant to businesses and individuals on all aspects of their communication.

PREFACE

by Frank Foley

As the world emerges from Covid-19, increasingly, people are sharing stories of "silver linings" from the pandemic, including stronger bonds with family and community, a greater appreciation of good health and the benefits of self-improvement, and the adoption of modern technologies.

My silver lining during Covid was discovering a new network of outstanding non-Japanese Japan Country Managers thanks to the proliferation of online platforms and forums such as Clubhouse, podcasts, and YouTube channels during lockdown. These Country Managers came from various industries and locations around Japan. Listening to their insightful and revealing stories, I realized three things:

1. While the specifics often differed by industry, their challenges were very similar.

2. Their highly innovative solutions and successful outcomes were often industry-agnostic and could be applied in any business or company type.

3. Despite the importance of the Japanese market to so many foreign companies, nobody had written about all of this from the perspective of the Japan Country Managers themselves.

These Japan Country Managers were not the "charisma" celebrity business leaders held in such awe by the media, but people who mostly operate below the radar, quietly accumulating knowledge and insight, building their lives in Japan as valued members of their community and their company. I was astounded by the breadth and depth of their experience, by their clarity of perception and by the strength of their commitment. For any foreign company in need of direction in its Japan strategy, this non-Japanese resident business community represents a vast resource of know-how that is ready and waiting to be applied.

Someone needed to talk to these people and capture their stories!

Having lived and worked in Japan for 33 years, including 22 years as Country Manager, I was confident I could convince my peers to talk to me. I was less sure, however, in my ability to turn all these conversations into a book. So, I turned to my good friend and Japan-based corporate communications expert, David Pinsker, to plan the book's structure and take the lead on writing and editing. The process began by reaching out to our contacts, which quickly led to more introductions. We ultimately interviewed approximately 20 Japan Country Managers from diverse industries and careers, including movies, medical equipment, tourism, professional business services, and even a lawyer with additional degrees in philosophy and computer science. We wanted to learn about their challenges, solutions, success stories, and even failures. We structured the interviews around their experiences with key stakeholders: Japanese consumers, Japanese key partners, local management and staff, and their head office (and boss). We focused on the cultural aspects of local strategy, change leadership, staff engagement, key partner management, communication, building and maintaining trust, and head office/boss related issues.

The book comprises two sections. Part One is an overview written by the authors, which presents these and other themes from the interviews and also references relevant market data and other published works. Part Two is a collection of 13 edited transcripts of contributor interviews.

Who should read this book?

This book is for anyone interested in operating a successful *gaishikei* (foreign-owned company) in Japan. Whether you are an experienced Japan-hand or an aspiring newcomer, the stories from our contributors will deepen your understanding of doing business in Japan and possibly affirm what you already know. In addition to Country Managers themselves, we recommend this book to all head office executives who work with or will be working with them. This includes CEOs, heads of international, a wide range of departmental leaders, and most importantly, HR. Similarly, the book is highly relevant to Japan-based executives who interact with Country Managers such as their 2ICs, members of the local leadership team, local partners, and recruiters. We would also recommend this book to Japanese private and public sector executives, officials, academics, students, and journalists interested in the challenges faced by *gaishikei* and their contribution to the Japanese economy. While the book focuses primarily on foreign companies entering or already active in Japan, we also believe that it will interest Japanese companies engaged, or about to engage, in business with western counterparts. And finally, we would recommend it to anyone interested in culture and how it impacts every aspect of our behavior as professionals and consumers.

ACKNOWLEDGMENTS

We have to start by thanking all of the contributors to this book for taking the time to share their insightful and inspiring stories with us. In addition to the 13 people included in Part Two, we would also like to acknowledge the invaluable input, both directly and over long-term relationships, from advisors and other friends and colleagues including Jason Ball, Roger Berman, Benjamin Boas, Peter Byrne, Eric Cole, Mark Darbyshire, John Flanagan, Adam Fulford, Aiichiro Furukawa, David Gray, Dr. Joseph Haldane, Mary Ann Halford, Andrew Hankinson, Motonori Iwasaki, Yoshitsugu Koizumi, Rochelle Kopp, Alastair Lamond, John Lowe, Maya Matsuoka, Hamish Macaskill, John McBride, Goushi Nakano, Erika Ogawa-Arai, Ward Platt, Margaret Price, Ross Rowbury, Michael Ryan, Dr. Haruko Sato, Kazuhiro Shimada, Susumu Shimoyama, Tim Schultz, Paul Shepherd, Dan Slater, Alexander O. Smith, Bruce Steinberg, Greg Story, and Katsuhiko Waza. We would also like to thank three great storytellers - Tim Sullivan, Valerie Foley, and Mark Heppelle - for reading and providing invaluable feedback on the flow, clarity, and logic of an earlier draft of the book. The incredible creativity of our page and cover designer (and copy editor) Brian Smith is self-evident. We highly recommend Brian to anyone requiring such services.

DEDICATION

by Frank Foley

I would like to dedicate this book to my university mentor and renowned Japanologist, Professor Ross Mouer, who, even though I didn't understand it at the time, taught me that the first question is always "why?"

CONTENTS

PART ONE - AN OVERVIEW OF JAPAN COUNTRY MANAGEMENT

PART TWO - THE INTERVIEWS

- PART ONE -

AN OVERVIEW OF JAPAN COUNTRY MANAGEMENT

Introduction

The genba (現場)

Genba is a Japanese word that is gradually taking its place in the English business lexicon. The meaning is similar to the English expression "in the field" or "on the shopfloor", but with the added nuance of the challenges of real-world business. It points to the place where value-creating work actually occurs, as opposed to the simulation presented in a boardroom or represented in marketing plans or spreadsheets.

The *genba* is where we went to find out why international companies in Japan sometimes succeed admirably but, too often, quietly fail. We collected stories from over 20 Japan Country Managers from a wide range of industries, each with at least ten years' in-country management experience. We wanted to learn how they were able to apply their deep understanding of Japanese culture and business to tackle the many misconceptions and stereotypes about Japan and to develop practical and robust business strategies and solutions. We focused on westerners working at western-owned companies. Although there are also many Japanese managers of foreign-owned companies with important stories to tell, their career structure and the expectations placed upon them differ from those of non-Japanese Country Managers, and for this reason they are beyond the scope of this volume. Furthermore, we restricted ourselves to SMEs because we believe that the challenges and expectations placed upon Country Managers are also shaped significantly by company scale. [1]

We refer to them as "Japan-Insider Country Managers."

Japan country management today

The number of foreign-run small and medium-sized enterprises (SMEs) has been growing strongly since the early 1990s when Japan first eased restrictions on foreign companies. Between 2002 and 2019, the number of first-time senior-level business visa entrants per year quadrupled from 566 to 2,237. By 2019, cumulatively there were 27,249 people on senior management visas – and an unknown number of senior foreign executives on permanent resident visas (*eijuuken*). In 2020 there were an estimated 26,620 SMEs run by non-Japanese CEOs. [2]

Not only is the Japan Country Manager universe expanding, but, more importantly, the role and expectations are changing with a shift from head-office expats to Japan-savvy, culturally literate communicators. The changes were accelerated by Covid-related travel restrictions, but, as reported in The Economist recently, they were happening anyway. In an article entitled *End of the travelling circus: Who needs expats these days?,* The Economist observes that, for decades, dispatching expatriate executives was how international companies signaled their market priorities. But times have changed and the business case for expats has been weakening for years. Today, sending an expatriate western executive to a far-flung market is now seen as an outdated extravagance. "The surest way to signal commitment to a market these days is not by importing top talent but by nurturing it locally." The article concludes, "That isn't a reversal of globalism so much as affirmation of it." [3]

Speaking on *Japan Expert Insights* Clubhouse room, international business expert Frank Marton, echoed this point.

"(What makes a good international businessperson) ...has changed tremendously in the last few decades... In the 70s, 80s, and even in the 90s it was all about bringing some kind of know-how, and when a so-called "western businessperson" got off a plane there was this sort of automatic deference to the level of skills and know-how that they have. That has changed a tremendous amount as the world had gotten smaller, and information is available everywhere. So now I'm seeing that many times the (old style) expatriates from what we used to call the first-world countries are not the most successful (at international business) ...The world has moved on. (Rather than viewing the expat with deference) ...people are looking at you and thinking, well this person is probably going to be gone within 12 to 36 months, so is it worth my time to invest to get to know them. Successful foreign businesspeople now, know that they need to listen, learn, build trust over time, and ultimately be able to offer Japan something that is both different and appealing." [4]

Cultural understanding is another critical requirement of today's Japan Country Managers. According to one of the most highly regarded experts on doing business in Japan, Ross Rowbury, "It is no longer good enough just to explain "what" is different about Japan, but more importantly "why" the difference exists, and "how" it impacts business behavior." Country Managers must be able to see through the myriad of misconceptions and stereotypes about Japan and create solutions based on real understanding. Rowbury shared an example of a recent Japan/US conference call on a joint project. "After the call I was asked by the US side why the Japan side didn't "speak up." The implication was that innate Japanese politeness was impeding communication. But as any experienced Japan-hand will know, the behavior that the US side perceived as politeness was actually due to the very different styles of communication typical in low- and high-context cultures. In a low-context culture such as the US, the speaker will check repeatedly that the listener has understood their point by saying the same thing in different ways. In a high-context culture like Japan, the speaker would normally just make a point once and be confident that the broader (unspoken) meaning is implied. In this instance, the US side's multiple explanation actually confused the Japanese side because they thought each one had some significance."

Of course, there will always be specific contexts where an old-style expat will still be the best option for a company. For example, in a startup scenario, where knowledge transfer from the parent/group companies is important, or where its business is highly specialized and the internal learning curve so steep that only a company insider can match the specifications. An expat might also be the appropriate choice in more extreme cases where the mandate is to enforce drastic change through shock and awe tactics, such as in the infamous case of Carlos Ghosn at Nissan. [5]

But these are very specific situations and are usually short-term solutions. For most companies, the job of the Country Manager is to lead change in a cross-cultural environment.

This requires core "Japan Insider" skills including cultural empathy, verbal and non-verbal communication, strong external networks and a solid reputation. It requires the ability to build and maintain trust internally and externally. Japan-Insider Country Managers with this real-life experience may need time and support to learn head office goals and strategy but can hit the ground running (at a Japan-appropriate pace).

Japan-Insider Country Managers are "in Japan, but not of Japan." They bring an additional perspective compared to those whose life experience is shaped only by Japanese cultural norms and references. Beyond their Japanese-language and cultural communication skills, they add a foreign/head office perspective which often results in innovative and unexpected solutions. We contend that the accumulated insight and expertise of the resident non-Japanese business community is a highly valuable but under-utilized resource waiting to be monetized, as these stories will demonstrate. [6]

Is Japan for you?

We often hear about how difficult Japan is for foreign companies. Despite major investment and strong local partnerships, several major players have come and gone with their tail between their legs. High profile examples in the retail sector include Walmart, the world's largest bricks-and-mortar retailer, UK supermarket giant Tesco, and high-street favorite Boots the Chemists.

Walmart, despite what was widely regarded as a smart strategy, eventually sold its majority stake in Seiyu and exited the market. [7] Tesco admitted defeat in 2011, after spending more than £250 million over eight years trying to establish a business at scale in the country. [8] Boots' tie-up with Mitsubishi Corporation ended in 2001 with £25 million in losses after just two years of operation. [9] A spokesperson at the time blamed the company's failure to understand Japanese lifestyle. [10] Carrefour, the French hypermarket, made the all-too-common mistake of going toe-to-toe against entrenched local competition before exiting in 2005. In fast foods, Burger King withdrew in 2001 due to poor performance after its first entry in the 1990s. It has since returned with the support of Lotte Korea, but sales remained sluggish, and even after Affinity Equity Partners acquired the Japanese operation in 2017, the number of stores remains only about 5% of those of McDonald's. [11] And in the cable and satellite TV sector, DirectTV exited in 2000 after only three years and huge expenditure. Rupert Murdoch's News Corp was unable to replicate its success in the US, UK, Australia and Hong Kong, and exited in 2005.

It is easy to point to regulatory and industry barriers as the cause, or to consumer and social attitudes, but the argument does not hold up as other brands, often in the same or similar sectors, have succeeded. A more robust explanation is that successful companies connected with Japanese consumers by offering products and services that were both different and appealing, and delivered them through a localized strategy. While anchored in the brand story and DNA of the parent company, they built a local strategy based on a deep understanding of the culture, lifestyle and needs of Japanese consumers.

Prominent success stories include McDonald's Japan, which reported operating profit for the fiscal year ended December 2020 of 30 billion yen ($285 million), up 10% from the previous year. Key elements of its local strategy include adopting a local menu with Ebi Filet-O and Teriyaki McBurger. They also adjusted serving sizes, and selected shop locations based on Japanese lifestyle, and were quick to add salads when there was a spike in adverse publicity regarding obesity. They responded nimbly to Covid by adding online ordering and delivery, increasing ARPU by 17%. [12] [13]

Illustrating how effectively McDonald's has inserted itself into the Japanese consumer landscape, a Japanese friend of the author tells how his seven-year-old son, seeing the golden arches logo on his first trip to the US, remarked in amazement that "they have McDonald's here, too, Dad."

Since launching in 1998, Amazon Japan has grown rapidly, and Japan is the third-largest international market after Germany and the UK. The business, covering a huge range of product categories and SKUs, has grown by more than seven-fold since 2010 from ¥43.7 billion (US$401 million) to ¥3.2 trillion ($24.3 billion) in 2022 or 4.7% of Amazon's global revenue. [14] This is hardly surprising since, in many ways, Japan is the perfect market for Amazon. Japan has an extensive and well-developed home delivery network, as the *ukiyoe* (woodblock prints) from the Edo era (1603~1868) bear testimony. [15] Even today, 95% of daily newspapers are home-delivered [16], and 21 *takkyubin* courier services deliver 355 million items every month. [17]

Ikea withdrew and researched extensively after the failure of its "one-size-fits-all" approach from 1974-1986 and relaunched in 2006 very successfully simply by taking Japanese customer needs as its starting point. This made a radical difference in its selection and size of stores and the range of goods they offered, as well as the services it provided, such as assembly and delivery. [18]

Costco offered a new model not met by Japanese retailers (as opposed to Carrefour, which positioned itself in competition with Japanese retailers). [19] Starbucks completely re-imagined the coffee-shop, taking an unashamedly foreign brand and giving it unparalleled exposure. One of its early innovations in 1996 was to establish the no-smoking rule in its cafes, at a time when smoking was still the norm in Japanese cafes. They offered a stylish, bright and relaxing environment incorporating Japanese customer service as a core part of its brand. Starbucks' recent collaboration with the books and media distributor Tsutaya (T-Sites) takes that concept even further. [20]

While there is no single path to success, these and many other successful if less well-known cases all have something in common in how these businesses approached Japan.

Whether a new market entrant or a turn-around situation, in all successful cases the company did its homework. It took the time and effort to understand Japan in a broad sense - not just its own market segment, but the industry and the regulatory and economic landscape, social structures and attitudes, demographics and consumer behavior, wants and needs. With this knowledge, the successful company did not simply try to "slot" its product in; they asked themselves some searching questions about their product, how it might be used in Japan, and by whom. They had to be objective about the product and be prepared to make changes if necessary. On that basis, the company could then set out its strategy and organization, and identify the management, the partners and supporters that would deliver the desired outcome.

Whatever strategy or organization was decided on, the successful companies showed commitment, built trust, and had the organizational flexibility to act within the Japanese business environment. In other words, they were prepared to "leave their silos at home." Successful companies trusted and empowered their local teams in Japan.

The Big Picture

As noted above, today's Japan Country Manager must understand the cultural side of business and be able to apply that to strategy and decision-making. A recurring message from contributors, in this regard, was the importance of the larger context - including the social contract, the employment model, and other key characteristics of the labor market.

The social contract

Japan, they say, is governed by a social contract whereby individuals accept the discipline of society in return for security. Engaging in risky or disruptive behavior can result in loss of that security, or even expulsion from the group. One contributor explained it in terms of different approaches to problem solving:

"At the root of every society, everybody has at the back of their mind the final consequence. In the American context it's usually the sheriff, which is a gun. You will be removed, forcefully if necessary. Somebody is going to show up with a gun to enforce what is collectively desired.

In Japan that force element has been shrunk to basically just anti-social and criminal elements, who don't appear to do it very well! The consequences in Japan are exclusion from the circle, leading to things like overwhelming depressive shame, which is pretty bad. Everybody wants to be liked by everybody else at the end of the day, so, if you don't want to be homeless and shunned, you follow the rules."

Others explained the social contract in terms of Japan's historical relationship with rice. Traditionally, labor-intensive wet rice cultivation has always been a high-risk endeavor. Japan's mountainous terrain meant that land was scarce, so resources needed to be shared to achieve scale. Moreover, the concentrated planting window meant the cooperation of the entire community was needed. Facing the constant threat of typhoons, earthquakes, and pests, the consequences of failure were dire. Physical survival literally depended on communal resource usage. It is no surprise, therefore, that this gave rise to a culture of cooperation, with families pooling labor and sharing water resources and irrigation facilities. It also resulted in a rules-based culture, with severe consequences such as exclusion for non-compliance. According to Adam Fulford, who explores the connection between traditional lifestyle and community resilience, "Selflessness and empathy which might tend to be associated with stereotypical perceptions of Japanese people as humble and self-effacing are actually very practical survival mechanisms based on maximizing utility." [21]

Ulrike Shaede borrows from social psychology to dig deeper into the high value placed on observance of "rules and process" in Japan. [22] Quoting research by Michele Gelfand that covered 33 countries, she argues that all cultures fall within a spectrum ranging from "tight" to "loose." "Tight" cultures tend to follow rules and processes, and value hierarchy. People tend to have a "sensitive social radar" whereby behavior is impacted by individual sensitivity to how the environment perceives them, and they place a high value on behaving correctly. For very practical reasons, countries prone to natural disasters are more likely to be "tight."

Unsurprisingly, Gelfand's research found that Japan falls at the tight end of the spectrum, but it is by no means alone or unique in this sense. Norway, Malaysia, India, Singapore, and

South Korea actually rank higher. The US and Australia are at the loose end, which tends to be more flexible, fluid, entrepreneurial, accommodating, and forgiving of deviation and failure.

The picture that emerges from contributors' observations and academic research is that Japan is a rules-based culture that places a high value on observing process, hierarchy, and following socially acceptable behavior. Conversely, there is little or no perceived upside to engaging in change.

The employment model

The traditional employment model, which was at its zenith in the post-war years of rapid growth and expansion, has been described as the victory of the tortoise over the hare. Although lifetime employment is now far from ubiquitous, the attitudes that underpin it remain widely in evidence in work practices, and astute Japan-Insider Country Managers will be aware of them. As one contributor observed:

"The Japanese employment model is slow, steady promotions, no superstars called out or paid that way. You're a tortoise and not a hare. And that's how the HR department will develop your career. It's how your compensation is going to increase. In order to make sure everyone is treated fairly and equitably, if everyone is treated as a tortoise, then nobody is ever caught out on anything."

The tight labor market

The Teikoku Databank's 2022 labor market survey showed that even Japanese companies are struggling to find employees. Over half of the 11,621 responding companies said that they faced a shortage of full-time employees. And the labor market can only be expected to tighten with increased demand driven by a rise in inbound and domestic tourism, and decreased labor supply due to the ongoing aging of the population. [23]

Furthermore, a 2021 study reported in *Japan Labor Issues* found that, even in a sellers' labor market, employees favor long-term continued service rather than job-hopping. While there is an emerging fluid employment sector, the market continues to show a tendency to long-term continued service, even among non-manufacturing enterprises. The reason, they conclude, is that the fluid employment sector typically offers lower wage levels than the long-term employment sector and does not offer opportunities for higher wage growth through job changes. [24]

The reality for foreign companies is that Japanese job seekers continue to favor long-term service with domestic companies. While foreign companies may benefit in the future from increasing labor fluidity, they need to work harder than their Japanese counterparts if they are to attract and retain high-quality Japanese staff.

How the Big Picture helps to understand doing business in Japan

Understanding the larger context described above helps explain apparent paradoxes, such as the following:

Why do Japanese employees score so low on engagement surveys?

How can it be that Japan - which we know as the home of *kaizen* (relentless pursuit of improvement [25]), superior customer service, excellent products and dedicated employees who work all hours and do not take their meager holiday allowance - scores so badly on global employee engagement scales? In one example, a 17-country study on recruitment, retention and engagement entitled *Winning Strategies for a Global Workforce*, Japan ranked bottom in terms of "engagement", with only 2% identifying as "highly engaged" vs. the global average of 14%. Japan was second highest in terms of "disengaged employees" at 41%. Only India had a higher percentage, and apart from India no other country had more than 29% of employees identified as disengaged. The global average was 24%. The study concludes that even taking cultural differences into consideration, Japan is an outlier on this scale. [26]

With their understanding of the larger social context, many of our contributors dismissed western-style engagement surveys as culturally inappropriate for Japan. That opinion is supported by the research. A cross-cultural study of the measurement accuracy of the Japanese and the original Dutch versions of the Utrecht Work Engagement Scale suggested that low Japanese scores might reflect decreased accuracy in the measuring scale of the Japanese sample, due to the Japanese tendency to suppress positive self-expression. Coupled with the high evaluation placed on self-enhancement in western societies, the study advised caution in drawing conclusions from current engagement scales, and recommended that new psychometric studies are needed for cross-cultural engagement measurement. [27] These findings were echoed in a more recent study focusing on Japan, which came to a similar conclusion stating that measuring employee engagement in Japan required a new theoretical system suitable for Japan, different from the western concept of social exchange theory. [28]

Are Japanese people really so risk-averse?

Chronic risk aversion is frequently quoted as the reason for everything from Japan's underdeveloped venture capital industry to the unwillingness of employees to speak up in meetings. This is not a view held by most Japan-Insider Country Managers and other cultural experts. Professor Almoamen Abdalla of the Tokai Institute of Global Education and Research argues that the Japanese word "*risuku*" and "risk" in English don't even mean the same thing. The Japanese word means "something dangerous that will lead to a negative outcome," in contrast to the English "risk" which contains a stronger sense of "a calculated act that will be a great success if it goes well." This calculation has at its heart the idea of gambling on a successful outcome. [29]

As pointed out by several contributors, it's not that Japanese are culturally more risk averse than anyone else, it's that the risk-to-reward equation in Japan is different. If a Japanese employee takes a risk and things go well, credit goes not to the individual, but to the company. If, on the other hand, things go badly, it's the individual's fault. There is no incentive to take risks.

According to Ross Rowbury, it is more useful to describe Japanese employees as "uncertainty averse." He says that what westerners often perceive as stubborn aversion to risk is actually just a request for more information, and importantly, the right type of information. The less uncertainty there is, the more employees are willing to try something new and embrace change. [30]

The key, then, is to understand the real concerns employees have about embracing change. Cross-cultural communications expert, Rochelle Kopp, tells a story of a U.S. subsidiary of a Japanese company who asked for her help. A new American marketing manager had been tasked with getting head office approval for a new locally designed product line in the USA. Despite being confident of acceptance by USA customers, the proposal had already been rejected twice by head office in Japan. When she examined their previous proposals, Kopp immediately spotted the problem. As is common in the west, the US side had focused on analysis of the present and future market and the predicted future demand, with no reference to potential lessons from the historical context. She writes,

"Japanese organizations often tend to be reluctant to go after fads, and instead would prefer to concentrate on things that have the likelihood of being enduring. Without information on how the market had behaved in the past, most likely the head office did not feel that the proposal was sufficiently grounded. It appeared that because they lacked the information they needed in order to feel comfortable, they rejected the proposal. Perhaps because they themselves had trouble putting their finger on what was missing, they did not give a clear explanation. Once the historical information was added and other enhancements made to the proposal... it was approved." [31]

Why is Japan so non-litigious?

It is often remarked that Japan is a non-litigious society. Japan has only about 1/10 the number of lawyers per person compared to the US, and the state of Maryland alone has about the same number of lawyers as the whole of Japan. [32] Several years ago, in expectation that Japan would see a surge in lawsuits, the Justice Ministry initiated a very successful program which increased the number of lawyers in Japan from 22,021 in 2006 to 43,104 as of September 2021. But lawsuits did not increase, partly due to Covid, but mostly due to the non-litigious culture, and Japan's ongoing population decline. The focus now is on reducing the number of new lawyers allowed to sit the bar exam. [33]

This is not to say that companies and people do not fall out, or that some disputes don't end up in court. But the comparative rarity of corporate litigation, and the much lower profile of corporate legal departments in Japan, suggest that companies do not rely on legal recourse to determine how and with whom they conduct business. Instead, according to some of our contributors, companies place a greater emphasis on group affiliations and identity. In other words, whether a person or a company is perceived to be "inside the circle" is the determining factor.

What happens if you are not inside the circle? In an example from the character and brand-licensing business, when a popular foreign kids' brand was abruptly dropped by one of Japan's largest national free-to-air TV channels, the broadcaster simply evoked a tenuous technical clause in the contract. In another example, a US-licensed attorney at a major Japanese law firm saw a Japanese company unceremoniously abandon negotiations with a foreign partner and acquire a rival company. The US side had negotiated in good faith and followed all the cultural advice about allowing the Japanese side to take its time to reach a decision and was completely blindsided by this move.

It seems that in both cases this could happen because the foreign partner was perceived to be outside the circle. Another contributor went further: "This is the same logic by which an otherwise humanitarian and empathetic Japan can refuse to allow refugees into the country," he commented.

Examples like these may give the impression of an insurmountable yet invisible barrier to foreign Japan Country Managers. That is not our view, but we do stress that they must win the support and trust of all Japanese stakeholders, both internal and external, to have any hope of success.

Many observed that trust in Japan takes a long time to build, especially for a non-Japanese boss, and can be lost in an instant. One contributor added that this is especially true for Country Managers who are coming in fresh. "It's so easy to isolate the Country Manager from the company, especially if the Country Manager has a time limit like one or two or three years. It takes a lot of immersive work to get inside the circle, and, even then, the door can be slammed shut by one bad move."

Echoing similar sentiments, another contributor described the situation when he was hired as the Japan Country Manager for a global advertising agency. "The two big issues I noted were lack of trust between staff and management, and amongst staff themselves." This would be a problem in any situation, but is even more acute in today's competitive labor market, where acquisition and retention of high-quality staff is a huge challenge, especially for foreign companies.

Why is English-language proficiency so low in Japan?

Language seems to present a bigger problem in Japan than in most other non-English speaking markets. Japan consistently ranks low on English-language proficiency indices, and interest in living or working abroad is limited and declining. [34] This contrasts sharply with Asian neighbors such as South Korea, Taiwan, and China where overseas exchanges and work postings are highly sought after. The reason is simple: motivation. Most Japanese people do not perceive a need to venture overseas or to learn a foreign language in order to enjoy a high quality of life. [35] Japan has economic scale, the food is delicious, and everything works!

Given that English language proficiency is key to effective communication in global business, it is surprising how little attention companies place on strengthening language skills. In Japan, middle managers might be expected to have "business English" in their tool kit, and be required to dust it off in international dealings, but they are rarely fluent. Since these people are usually the primary communication channel, this is a very serious issue. Nonetheless, most companies "make-do" in this way, rather than hire professional interpreters or translators.

Worse still is when the foreign company does not have Japanese speakers on its staff and must also rely on the often sub-par English skills of its would-be partner. This puts both sides in an uncomfortable position. For the foreign company, even if things are going well, they cannot escape the feeling that they are "flying blind", unable to see for themselves what is happening and, more importantly, unable really to trust. For the Japanese side it is usually the hapless middle-manager assigned to manage the foreign business who takes on the additional burden of responsibility, and possibly the blame for any errors, all for no additional reward.

It is not uncommon for international companies to cast their bilingual Japan Country Manager in the role of interpreter. This is a grave error. Obviously, the manager can facilitate better communication, but should never be used in place of a professional interpreter. In meetings, the manager must be free to participate fully in discussions and negotiations, and to deploy his or her cross-cultural communication skills to read the meeting. It is impossible to do that and interpret at the same time.

It is essential to have a skilled interpreter in the room. Broadly speaking there are three options: The first, and best option if available to you, is to hire a dedicated in-house professional interpreter. This is obviously costly and only practical for large companies with full-time interpreting needs. The second, and more common option is to use a relatively junior member of staff who is not directly involved in the topic at hand. This is a good option in that they will be familiar with the subject matter, which helps both in terms of accuracy and strategy. It is important, however, that the company provides professional training for that employee. Being bilingual does not necessarily make an effective interpreter. It is a specialized skill and requires training and practice. The third option is to use a third-party professional interpreter, of which there are many in Japan.

How different is Japan?

"Japan is different" (JID) is one of the most overused and misused expressions that new Country Managers will encounter.

Most of the contributors we spoke to recounted several cases where this was the first response from their Japanese colleagues and partners to any new product idea or service introduced. One contributor, from the educational publishing field, had firsthand experience of a Japanese-national Country Manager who was convinced that global strategy didn't apply because "Japan is different." He took the company so far away from the company's global strategy that the parent company decided to shut down the Japan business and withdraw from the market entirely.

"JID" is a truism. It is true in itself, but its truth sheds no light on the situation. Quite the opposite, it merely reinforces old stereotypes and preconceived notions. This mentality is a far more intransigent problem than mere cultural misunderstanding. No doubt, the emissaries of transformational brands and concepts such as Starbucks, Amazon, smartphones and IMAX movies were also told initially that "Japan is different."

What IS different about Japan is the same thing that is different in any culture – its own unique historical and cultural context. As in any country, the Japan-Insider Country Manager will question "why," will challenge preconceived or ill-conceived notions, and will clear the ground on which to build a robust strategy.

How to build a local strategy

As noted above, successful companies take the time and effort to really understand Japan in a broad sense - the regulatory and economic landscape, social structures and attitudes, demographics and, most importantly, the consumer. They make brave decisions and bold changes if necessary, and focus on building trust with customers, partners and staff. In other words, they do their homework and build a robust local strategy based on that understanding.

Surpass consumer expectations

Japan's insistence on quality, service and presentation has been widely documented. Smart foreign companies learn how to build this into the culture of their Japanese entity, and, whenever appropriate, adopt best practices from Japan in other markets.

In an example from a global certification company, historically, the overseas head office had printed and mailed certificates to Japanese holders. The process seemed to work well, and the intention was to keep it in place even after the company opened their Japanese office. That quickly changed one day when the Japan office received a complaint from a certificate recipient about the poor state of the framed certificate she had received from the company's overseas head office. It seemed that, despite head office's best efforts, framed certificates were prone to damage in transit. Head office's initial reaction was that the damage was minimal and recommended issuing an apology and a replacement certificate to the customer. The manager takes up the story:

"However, with my Japan team on-board, we refused to be mollified. In a Japanese context, we understood that this was an

extremely serious customer service issue. We fully understood that a certificate represented a major life achievement for the recipient. Ensuring excellent service at all stages of the challenge process – including the delivery of a pristine certificate – was our most important job."

"While HQ immediately agreed that Japan should handle the preparation of certificates locally, we considered the matter serious enough to take a somewhat extreme step of introducing a "white gloves policy", much like a museum curator handling ancient artifacts, and created a dedicated area for the printing and packaging of certificates. Fully aware of the gravity of the issue, our team made further suggestions. One was to offer to re-issue certificates to existing certificate holders in Japan. Another was, whenever practical, for a uniformed company representative to hand-deliver the certificate. Even more, to create a sense of ceremony even when delivered by courier, we prepared branded packaging materials. The company came to see that its job was not limited to recording results and dispatching certificates; it had to be intimately involved in the customer experience. As a result, market opportunities expanded considerably as did customer interaction. And to HQ's credit, they began to appreciate the significance of what Japan was doing and adopted best practices where appropriate in other markets."

Understand what your product or service "does" for the Japanese consumer

Clayton Christensen, who was described by The Economist as "the most influential business thinker of his time," famously applied job theory to product development by asking "what do you employ this product to do?" He explains how his research team was able to help a restaurant increase sales of a milkshake, not by changing price or product features, but by understanding the "job" the milkshake performed in the lives of its customers. In this example, when asked why they "employed" a milkshake, customers responded that it was (1) easy to consume one-handed while driving, and (2) helped stave off hunger pangs until lunchtime. [36]

Speaking on Tim Romero's excellent podcast *Disrupting Japan*, UX/UI expert Brandon Hill makes a similar point with regard to Japanese websites. He talks about the danger of jumping to conclusions about "the job" Japanese consumers expect a website to perform. Romero puts it to Hill that "To western eyes, (Japanese websites are) just too busy, too dense, too confusing, too outdated, and just plain wrong... Japanese web design is broken." Hill acknowledges that there are some areas where western sensibilities might lead to improvement, but argues that there are several rational reasons for why Japanese web design is the way it is, not the least of which is that it's what the Japanese consumer wants. He says that they are used to the dense, busy design from print advertising, and they feel more comfortable with that online too. And they are not asking for change. [37]

Through our research and personal experience, we came across several instances of a product or service succeeding in Japan only after companies took the time to understand how they were perceived by Japanese consumers, and committed to a local strategy to deliver on their "job." In many cases, it was quite different from the original head office strategy.

Leave your silos at home

Too often, foreign companies fail in Japan because they are restricted by inflexible silo structures in their home country. To exploit emerging opportunities, foreign companies have to be flexible, not weighed down by corporate head office baggage.

Contributors from the entertainment industry talked about the "hubris of Hollywood" to illustrate a case of an industry imposing its home-country silos on Japanese and other international customers. Until relatively recently, the major Hollywood studios imposed tight control over the release sequence of their content through theatrical, home entertainment (DVD), and television sectors. The system, known as "windowing", ensured studios maximized revenues at every stage, and that executives continued to receive generous compensation packages and bonuses. [38] [39] Even in the face of the so-called "shut-in" (stay-at-home) economy - which emerged after the 2007-2008 global financial crisis where consumers were clearly demanding at-home services - the studios for the most part maintained their siloed windows. [40]

It took a global pandemic and the shuttering of theaters around the world, and the takeover of Hollywood by the big tech companies, to finally break through this Hollywood hubris and force them to bow to consumer demand for digital home release.

Contributors shared similar silo stories from other industries where they were instructed by head office to handover or sometimes completely abandon potentially lucrative deals simply to comply with head office structures. One example is from consumer publishing. In this case, the Japan-Insider Country Manager brought an opportunity to create a multi-media educational product with a major Japanese school and library publisher, using content from a US-based group company. However, he was instructed to abandon the project entirely, apparently because it fell outside the remit of his head office boss.

Be flexible and adaptable

A common characteristic of successful companies, on the other hand, is their flexible and adaptable approach to local strategy. Co-author Frank Foley shared two examples from his personal business experience of where such an approach by head office facilitated great success in Japan. The first example was Guinness World Records (GWR).

Despite being so ingrained in the Japanese psyche that *gine-su-kyuu* - meaning "the best" in Japanese - had become an adjective, book sales in Japan were low by GWR standards. The Japan team started to address this with traditional strategies - adding more local content, investing in marketing, even changing publishers, and so on. Sales grew, but they were still nowhere near enough to justify the costs of a local operation.

It wasn't until they stepped back and asked Clayton Christensen's "job" question that the solution emerged. It became clear that the opportunity to engage with Japanese consumers through a book was very limited. This was partly because there is no Christmas gift-giving tradition which underpins the majority of GWR book sales in western markets, and also because the book appealed to a narrow demographic of low-teen boys. To engage all demographics in Japan, GWR needed to be positioned as an experiential brand that was open to everyone. In other words, they needed to democratize being #1!

With the support of head office leadership, the Japan team developed an array of event concepts for communities, schools, and hospitals. They launched a nationwide program to support the revival of regional economies including supporting local artisans. They also ran commercially-sponsored events, marketing campaigns, and participated in TV shows. All events, regardless of who the customer was, were held to the same strict standards on record verification. The response was amazing. Over time, the "Japan strategy" was rolled out globally and is a major pillar of the company's business today. This would not have been possible without a company-wide commitment to finding the best local strategy for the brand in Japan.

The second example of finding a new job for the brand was National Geographic. National Geographic had long enjoyed high brand recognition and respect among older demographics in Japan through the National Geographic Magazine, the work of the National Geographic Society, and co-productions with Japanese broadcasters, including NHK. The Japan team at National Geographic Channel (NGC) spotted an opportunity to take the brand to a younger audience through English Language Learning (ELL). As former students themselves, they were aware that one of the biggest challenges facing English teachers in Japan was how to engage their learners, given the uninteresting and unnatural content of most existing textbooks. There was clearly an opportunity to bring the adventure, discovery and inspiration of National Geographic into the ELL classroom by creating reading, listening, writing, and speaking materials based on the brand's massive archive of videos, images and text.

The NGC team also knew that global ELL publisher Cengage Learning was already working with CNN using news clips, meaning that they already understood the value of branded content. With the help of Cengage's Japan office, they invited the publisher's senior editors for AsiaPac to National Geographic Channel's Tokyo office and pitched the idea. Cengage loved the concept and, thanks to a lot of hard work by the people at Cengage, a range of titles and products was subsequently rolled out as a global publishing program. Now known as National Geographic Learning, their graded readers and other teaching materials were an industry game-changer and are considered the benchmark for engaging ELL materials even today, with reported annual sales of $140 million.

Understand and leverage your special connection with Japanese consumers

The East India Company (EIC) is an example of a local Japan strategy that leverages the brand's special connection with Japan. EIC has possibly the longest associations of any foreign brand with Japan, at 410 years! It enjoys universal brand recognition in Japan because every schoolchild learns about the company's role in establishing trade and diplomatic relations between Japan and Great Britain in 1613. Gifts exchanged between the Tokugawa Shogunate and King James are still displayed proudly in both countries. And importantly, the introductions and mediation between EIC and the Tokugawa Shogunate was handled by the much-revered Miura Anjin (William Adams), made famous by Richard Chamberlain's portrayal in the movie, *The Shogun*. After over 150 years of dormancy, the company was acquired by Mumbai-born, London-based businessman, Sanjiv Mehta, in 2004 and relaunched in 2010. EIC currently has over 400 fine foods and beverages, from its core tea range to condiments, chocolate, coffee, confectionery, and, most recently, gin. But it was late to market in Japan and faced stiff competition from several established premium tea brands. Although the company has been distributing product in Japan for several years, as with GWR and National Geographic, revenue from Japan is small relative to its brand awareness.

To make a mark, EIC needed to establish a link between its universal brand awareness and its products and services, and to do this in a way that set it above the incumbent competition and appealed to Japanese consumers. As the company that brought tea to the western world, and that initiated international trade for the isolationist Tokugawa *bakufu*, the company's "job" was to deliver authentic and engaging stories and knowledge about tea, rather than sell product *per se*. At the time of writing, EIC was in the process of relaunching in Japan based on a combination of imported and locally licensed products in collaboration with a Japanese fine food partner. [41]

Local relevance and voice

Many contributors talked about the importance of creative flexibility to make the connection with Japanese consumers. One of the most well-known examples from publishing is Sidney Sheldon who, in the 1980s, achieved best-seller status in Japan by allowing a more interpretative style of translation. It was so successful that it spurned a new Japanese word – *chouyaku* – meaning "super-interpretative translation."

Another method used by foreign publishers to engage reluctant readers is to add a foreword or postscript by a local expert/ celebrity. Taking this a step further, some publishers and authors have localized the story itself to increase relevance for Japanese readers. A good example is the Japanese version of National Geographic's book, *Animal Ark,* which was recreated with original Japanese poetry by award-winning American-born, Japanese-language poet Arthur Binard. [42] Another interesting example is Harlequin, which publishes *manga* versions of its romance series in both print and digital formats.

Skillfully adding a Japanese character to entertainment properties is another way to make the local connection. The Japanese editor of the popular series *Alfie The Doorstep Cat* worked with the UK-based author to introduce a Japanese character, "Hana", to the series which opened up exciting content and promotional opportunities. In an early encounter between the streetwise London-born Alfie and the indoor cat Hana from Tokyo, they realize that cats everywhere are bound by their mission to comfort and protect their owners in times of need. That simple technique opened the door to potentially expand the franchise to friends from countries around the globe.

Another example of introducing a Japanese character into an overseas franchise is the much-loved children's property Thomas and Friends. Despite competition from local hero *Anpanman* in the unforgiving kids' market, Japan has long been one of the most successful non-English language markets for Thomas. At the time owned by HIT Entertainment, Thomas and Friends was already a very strong brand in Japan thanks to a long-running weekly slot on Fuji TV, excellent work by the local master licensee, Sony Creative Products (SCP), and a local HIT Entertainment team. But benchmarked against market leader, *Anpanman*, it was evident that Thomas could secure at least an additional 5% market share.

The Japanese Thomas team already had experience with localization strategies including launching the first Thomas Land outside the UK at the Fujikyu Highland Theme Park in Yamanashi, creating a new fixed attraction Thomas Town at the Shin-Misato Shopping Center just outside Tokyo, and a branded retail "shop-in-shop" concept called "Thomas Station" at numerous locations nationwide. It also extended the brand to the "baby" category with a cuter, softer design; and even employed Thomas in toilet training!

But without doubt the most important initiative was the introduction of a Japanese character to the world of Thomas. In collaboration with SCP and Japanese licensees, HIT Japan proposed to head office the introduction of a local character into the franchise. As with all Thomas characters, the Japanese character was based on an actual train model, in this case the D51, which is known as the steam locomotive that helped power Japan's early 20th-century economic development.

Introducing any new character into a global franchise such as Thomas and Friends is not easy. Introducing the first "foreign" character adds a further complication. One challenge was that, from a Japanese perspective, to be authentic, the D51 had to be black. But for non-Japan markets, black-colored merchandise does not sell well. Ultimately, however, thanks to some highly creative people at HIT head office, a character backstory was devised to resolve the color issue.

Another issue was the name. Initially the Japan side were very keen on older Japanese names harking back to the D51's golden era in the early 20th century, but overseas markets needed a name that worked everywhere. Eventually the name

Hiro was settled on - close enough to the English "hero" to be familiar to international audiences. The most important part of a character in Thomas' world – the face – was left to last. Early designs from head office would not work in Japan for various reasons and it seemed for a while that it might be impossible to agree on an image that would be acceptable both in Japan and internationally. The *eureka* moment came one day when one of the Japan team was watching a hit Hollywood movie starring an internationally recognized Japanese actor. He shared a face shot of the actor and received almost instant approval from both Japanese partners and head office. That face was the model for Thomas' new friend Hiro.

By adding Hiro, the Thomas franchise opened up exciting new storylines and merchandising opportunities including a 3D theater at Thomas Land Japan, and a "Day Out With Thomas (and Hiro)" annual summer event on the Oikawa Line in Shizuoka.

Local Partners - relationship-building and communication

For a foreign company, the top priority with partners is relationship-building. If you are not prepared to invest in that, maybe Japan is not for you. The responsibility for building and enhancing viable partner relations rests with the Country Manager. Building effective partner relations is a continuous process that does not always bring immediate quantitative results, and consequently is not prioritized. More than just seeing the other side's point of view, it calls for understanding what lies behind their negotiating positions. These skills are in addition to the product and industry knowledge needed to get the job done. Expat managers who are "parachuted in" to the position are unlikely, we contend, to have these vital "soft skills" to fulfill the role.

Assume that there will be miscommunication

A good starting point, according to one of our contributors, is to assume from the outset that there will be miscommunication. She was engaged by a Japanese company to support negotiations with a US firm in a joint bid to the US military. The Japanese side owned highly advanced technology that the American manufacturer was keen to incorporate, so there was a strong willingness for the two companies to cooperate. They needed to figure out how to partner, how to go after the bid, and how responsibilities would be divided. There were a lot of meetings, but both companies had their own very different attitude towards how they managed them. The Japanese were not in the habit of recording their meetings, so mostly they would report based on written-up comments, which were often incomplete. The US side relied on and expected verbatim recordings, and they became frustrated when the Japan representative reported back to them on meetings held between Japanese parties.

In her own words:

"There was so much miscommunication that the US side actually started thinking that the Japanese side were lying to them... The first thing I realized was that very little was being recorded in minutes or even emails. It was all verbal. What emails did exist were just exchanging pleasantries like 'The meeting went so well,' so everything looked positive and constructive. So the US side would say 'OK, good, go back and ask them for their quotation.' In one email, the Japan-based representative of the US company wrote, 'Dear Mr. Tanaka, As agreed, can you get us the estimate by tomorrow so we can clear this with our head office and take it forward.' Tanaka-san's response, of course, was 'No, we never said that!'"

To repair this breakdown in communication, both sides needed to be made aware of their own signals – verbal and non-verbal – and how the other side might interpret or misinterpret them. To the US side, this meant explaining that saying "*hai*" and "nodding" does not always mean "yes" and is in many cases an acknowledgement of what the speaker has said, not an agreement to it. To the Japanese side it also involved expanding their repertoire of communicative skills, so that they could more confidently ask for clarification, ask for more time, or restate their position.

It was also important to remind the US side that their Japanese counterparts, even if they were competent English speakers, were not using their native language, and that it would be reasonable to make some allowance for this.

While the US side insisted on sound recordings of meetings, they did not appreciate being presented with written minutes.

They seemed to regard this as unnecessary at best – since there should be a recording, and everybody knows what happened – and insulting at worst since everybody present was expected to sign off on the minutes. She cautioned that such an attitude is unfortunate, because minutes, if properly recorded and maintained, are an efficient low-maintenance way to keep track of what was said and what was decided.

Generally, in Japan, the practice of minuting remains intact for formal meetings. Several contributors encouraged foreign companies to prioritize Japanese-style minuting, not only in formal and external meetings, but also as a chat record for small and spontaneous meetings, internal or external, when anything is decided. This is even more valuable if you are communicating across different language and cultural spheres. Better collaborative software, and a more relaxed attitude in Japan towards document sharing, is making it more feasible.

Ultimately, it comes down to a fundamentally different attitude towards the purpose of meetings. For westerners, a meeting is a place to address problems and hammer out solutions, and agree on detailed action points. For Japanese, the purpose of a meeting is to produce a formal status report confirming what had already been agreed in other sessions.

Tactfully challenging assumptions and conventional wisdom

Common to successful Japan-Insider Country Managers is their willingness to challenge the status quo in ways that local teams cannot do. In Japan, not questioning established rituals and routines is a bedrock of society's rule-based stability. This same reticence to question assumptions, however, can restrict enterprise and innovation.

With this mindset, one contributor, who was an expert in cross-cultural project management, used her insights to challenge an accepted practice in her industry: time-consuming consensus building on very time-sensitive projects. She observed that the problem was particularly prevalent in what she called "soft projects", for example idea-based projects. Her solution was simple. She knew that project management in Japanese manufacturing, unlike "soft projects", was renowned for its efficiency and quality and has taught the world the value of *kaizen* (relentless pursuit of improvement) and *monozukuri* (the art, science and craft of making things) [43]. So her simple but elegant solution was to treat soft projects as if they are a manufacturing job with clear milestones and deadlines.

Another contributor from the publishing industry talked about how he challenged conventional wisdom on discount rates. In his own words,

"The standard industry discount in Japan was 35% and every company, including the foreign publishers, offered that. There was no question it was high and needed to be challenged. The Japanese publishers' position was 'we can't ask for a change, it's always been like that!' On the other extreme, there were publishers from outside the region who sent their regional guy in to hammer on the table and demand the same discount they were getting in the US. Our approach fell in the middle. We negotiated a smaller change but also had them add extra value such as a marketing or promotion commitment.

In my view, if you challenge the assumptions in a sensitive way, and show that you understand the market, people will engage and you will achieve the best result."

Local staff

Start by listening

Good managers know how to listen, and also how to show that they listen. In any new situation, our contributors recommended spending up to three months listening to staff at all levels. The manager needs to establish direct communication with middle- and lower-level staff without causing friction with senior managers. This is challenging in any culture, but even more so in a hierarchical society like Japan. To achieve this, contributors recommended several strategies including engaging HR as a strategic partner, and creating natural opportunities to interact directly with staff at all levels.

Partnering with HR

HR has an important strategic role to play in bringing about change, such as softening hierarchical structures, which is a challenge at many Japanese companies. According to Haruka Ishida, Consultant at Hays Japan,

"Traditionally, HR in Japan was very operational and largely revolves around payroll, social insurance, attendance reports etc. But recently organizations have started to realize HR can have a strategic role in areas such as client management or organizational development."

She explains that this is being driven by the 2018 "Work Style Reform Legislation" which has led to an increased demand for what she refers to as "strategic HR Business Partners (HRBP) who can help drive institutional change from the top." [44]

In an ever-tightening labor market, many companies are prioritizing staff retention through strategic HRBP. The 2021 *Survey of Trends in Business Activities of Foreign Affiliates* found that 54% of respondents identified "difficulties in securing human resources" as a growth inhibitor in Japan, second only to "high cost of doing business" (75.1%). Ishida also picks up on this point. She says that job hopping used to be seen as a bad thing, but, recently, companies are open to hiring candidates who switched jobs after as short as three years. "Younger workers are very happy to resign if they feel they are not being evaluated properly or don't see a career plan." Ishida concludes that HRBP is critical in fending off competitors from stealing your best people.

A marketing and communications professional explained how he worked with HR to avert a potential walkout of talented staff:

"I found two big staff-related issues. One issue was widespread lack of trust - in the company, between staff and management, and among staff themselves. The other issue was inappropriate allocation of skills to tasks. For example, account managers were doing copywriting, copywriters and designers were managing client expectations. There was no system, and there was no evaluation process, so nobody knew what they were supposed to be doing. This was odd because our company globally was actually very strong in this respect.

So, the first thing I did was build a robust evaluation system. I talked to every employee, every manager, to find out what their hopes were and what their clients' expectations were. I'd do a preliminary evaluation and I'd say, "Over the next three months, try to achieve this, and over the next six months try to achieve this, and we'll look at how far you've succeeded on those at the end of the year to determine what your assignment should be, and what your salary should be." It was complicated by the fact that, due to bad business results, the previous leadership had cut everybody's salary and then promised to reinstate it - when a certain point was reached - but this never happened. But it meant that after six months I was able to have a reassessment. I adjusted the goals because some of them were just not as achievable as they seemed six months earlier when they were set. This reassessment gave clarity of expectation and clarity of path forward to staff who did not have the benefit of either robust western HR practices, or the vaguer but implicitly understood Japanese practices.

The next step in getting people to stay with the company was to enthuse them about going through the (company) training programs... but they needed to be tailored to the Japanese environment. Localizing the training programs took a long time, and it was a continuous process. You could never take your eye off the ball. Because if you did – and it happened to me a few times at this company – things would get bogged down in a rigid western template style of managing staff. Or they'd spin off out of control. I ensured that new people coming into the company understood that this was the way things worked, and these were the expectations."

Creating opportunities for natural communication

Many contributors referred to the importance of spontaneous contact with staff at all levels. For example, "walking the halls" becomes part of the regular routine, so stopping at anyone's desk for a casual chat becomes a non-threatening, natural part of your presence. One contributor mentioned that he created time for this by reducing scheduled meetings from the default one hour to 30 minutes and using the unused meeting time to interact with staff. Similarly, making a point of visiting trade events or retailers where you can interact naturally with junior staff was highly recommended.

Frank Foley shared a story of how his head of HR at a publishing company created an opportunity for him to communicate with staff at all levels from day one. She sent out a note to all staff telling them that he was new to the area and would like to experience new restaurants for lunch. She asked them to form groups of 3~4 people (ideally from different departments) and take him to their favorite restaurant. It was a very effective way of allowing him to talk directly with even junior employees in a way that didn't make their bosses feel uneasy.

"For example, I learned about one junior manga editorial assistant who had plucked up the courage to apply for her current job despite having no qualifications, but 100% passion. I asked her to record the minutes of our lunch meeting in manga form which she later got to present at an all-staff meeting soon after. I could see from the reaction of the other staff that I wasn't the only one to be learning about her hidden talent for the first time. Another was a junior salesperson who had designed and launched a highly innovative marketing campaign with a national book chain to promote translated fiction titles. I also learned that the interpreter who had been employed to support the previous expat Japan Country Manager, a role no longer required, was actually a highly skilled digital marketer, a role we desperately needed to fill.

Just the act of talking directly with people was a step towards engaging them in the new plan, but more important was for me to show that I had listened through my actions. I made careful notes about their jobs, their ideas for change and improvement, and their challenges and concerns. For example, one frequent comment was that they had very little information about goals and strategy outside their own department. So, in consultation with the leadership team, we created what we called a "Hall of Fame" which was an actual hallway where each department displayed visual real-time updates. On the last Friday of each month, each department presented the projects they were working on."

Score some quick wins

Newly appointed Japan Country Managers typically arrive with ambitious plans, they are greeted by great expectations, and probably face a monumental task. Using the momentum of the appointment to garner some quick wins can pay dividends.

One co-author shares a story of how he leveraged his network to score a quick win.

"I had just been appointed Japan Country Manager for a global publisher. Although I had experience in publishing, I knew I still had to work to win the trust of the local team. During talks with staff, I learned that one of our challenges as a foreign company was access to high-profile Japanese authors. Thanks to previous mass media positions, I had quite a strong network in Japanese entertainment and sports. It was just before the 2018 FIFA World Cup, so I started with soccer. Top of my list was a player on the Japanese national soccer team who played his club football in England. While normally impossible for a Japanese publisher of our size to secure such a high-profile author, we came up with the idea of offering him simultaneous publication of his book in Japanese and English. He loved the idea, and we signed a contact almost immediately. For him, the

advantage was a book in English from a prestigious international publisher to tell his story to English football fans. For the company, by turning our "foreignness into an advantage, we could get a book from a high-profile Japanese celebrity that we could never hope to access otherwise. And for me personally, I went a long way towards gaining the trust of the team by delivering on a high-profile deal."

Softening the hierarchy

Rigid hierarchy can present a formidable obstacle to necessary change. Hierarchical structures are a fact of corporate life, and it is probably not possible or even desirable to break them down. But there are ways that they can be softened.

One approach is to set up project teams organized around skill sets rather than departments or position. In an example from the publishing industry, the answer was to create cross-departmental, book-specific project teams. The sole membership criterion was knowledge of and/or passion for the subject. Team leaders were chosen based on subject expertise. For example, the project leader for a book on Elon Musk's Tesla came from the IT department because he was an avid car fan with a special interest in electric vehicles. The leader on a health and wellness title was a mid-level finance person who was a dedicated yoga practitioner and health enthusiast. With very few exceptions, the reaction from all participants, at all levels, was very positive, as was the resulting sales performance of the books.

Another contributor used workshops structured around a specific business or organizational need. The workshops provided a natural, non-threatening forum to interact with staff at all levels, without hierarchical constraint. Within the workshops, the participants were exposed to instant feedback on how their own communication was conveyed and interpreted, providing an objective insight that would never be possible in the normal working environment. In this way, they learned that communication is a transaction in which both parties – the party giving the information and the party receiving it – have a responsibility for its safe transfer.

"By the end of the process, both sides have re-stated and re-confirmed and re-formed, and come to an agreement about what it is they are talking about. The challenge is that Japanese people are not as accustomed to doing workshops as western people are. So, you have to make it very non-threatening, very friendly, with lots of breakouts where it's two people talking to each other before they have to speak to the whole group."

According to our contributor, this led steadily to a general improvement in individual employees' communication skills, and also created new channels of communication as, in many cases, a lasting rapport was established among workshop participants.

Dealing with interdepartmental disconnect

A common problem in Japanese companies is an almost invisible disconnect between departments. On the surface it looks like they are communicating; there are meetings and emails and memos where information is being transmitted. Ultimately, however, decisions are often made internally in each department without reference to the bigger picture.

In one example from a publishing company, the result was that editorial was setting print-runs far in excess of reasonable sales forecasts, in order to justify production costs, which was obviously not sustainable. The reason for this behavior was clear:

lack of clear "ownership" of the print run allowed both sides to deflect responsibility to the other. The situation was exacerbated by conflict between the heads of both departments which long preceded the Country Manager's tenure.

The solution in this case was to make information and ownership transparent, and to celebrate success. There were three elements to the plan, all designed at achieving sustained change in behavior. The first was to build a product pipeline identifying all the decision points and all of the numbers - revenue projections and costs - for each product in the pipeline, and specifying who would sign off at each point. The second was to create a "Hall of Fame," which was literally a hallway where each department posted updates on the pipeline such as product packaging, print runs, on-sale dates and sales forecasts. And the third was to institute a regular "show-and-tell" session on the last Friday of every month, where the team member who actually did the work (irrespective of seniority level) reported on progress and results. And to make sure it really became part of the company culture, this was followed by a staff party where high-performing or notable team members were recognized.

Go to bat for the team

The most effective way to win the trust of the Japan team is a concrete demonstration of a readiness to argue – and preferably win – Japan's business case. Here are three stories where Japan-Insider Country Managers were highly effective advocates for Japan's business case, with very positive results:

Nike - everybody is an athlete

Our contributor explained that Nike was very serious about establishing and maintaining its athletic credentials, which was in its DNA. But it was also seen as having grown up in the shadow of Adidas which, as the makers of the original football boot, were seen as owning the serious athletics segment. Nike, on the other hand, was recognized as the "running footwear" brand. Nike Japan, however, could see that there was an opportunity in casual footwear, but realized this would be difficult to pitch to their head office people. Nike's head office shoe team were all athletes themselves - there were even world-champion runners on staff! - who considered it their ultimate priority to answer the needs of serious athletes.

Nike Japan's solution was to nurture, over a period of about three or four years, a redefinition of what an "athlete" was. The outcome was that they were able to create shoes that an athlete, or even a non-athlete, would find comfortable just walking around town in as casual shoes.

"So, over time, we got the marketing team around to the definition of "athlete" being: "if you have a body, you're an athlete." Initially there was some resistance to that, and a great deal of resistance around marketing because there was concern that doing something that looks more like fashion would damage Nike's athletic credentials. But to Nike's credit they tried it. It worked, and it didn't dent their athletic credentials in the areas where they were strong like running and basketball.

We launched a product called the Nike Presto... It was so successful in Japan that Uniqlo eventually copied it!"

Backing local instincts

A contributor from the international tourism industry shared two examples of when he needed to advocate on behalf of his Japanese team. In one example, head office was pushing back on Japan's plan to use Spotify, an audio platform, as the main promotional channel for a high-end video campaign. The logic on the Japan side was that the video series had an immersive sound feature which they thought was best showcased on an audio platform. His team asked him to fight their case, which he did successfully. And his team's instincts were right, and Spotify was one of the best performing promotion channels on that campaign. In his second example, head office wasn't keen on a proposed competition with a travel magazine where people would actually pay the magazine ¥5,000 to participate. They just didn't believe that anybody would participate. Again, the Japan-Insider Country Manager went to bat for the team, and, again, the Japan team's instinct was spot on, and the campaign was a huge success.

Winning new fans, keeping old ones

Star Wars Episode 1: The Phantom Menace was the first new installment in the franchise in 16 years since the original *Star Wars* trilogy, and Lucasfilm had very specific criteria for how the worldwide campaign should be conducted. While the Japan team at Fox understood these criteria, they also saw something more. They knew that Japan needed a customized strategy if it was to reach new audiences. The female audience quadrant, for example, was largely untapped but represented a huge potential interest that could be drawn in by the amazing costumes and fashion in the new film.

The Japan team also understood the importance of tradition and ceremony for Japanese fans, and wanted to incorporate it in the campaign. They proposed two large events each with 5,000 guests at Tokyo International Forum, where fans would watch interviews with the stars and special Japanese celebrity guests, and see fashion and martial arts presentations inspired by the movie. Initially, Lucasfilm were skeptical, believing the event would look like a simple publicity stunt and leave the audience unsatisfied. But for the Country Manager and the Japan team, the event was a gesture of respect and gratitude to their fans for their loyalty. They fought hard and were eventually given the green light.

The results were outstanding. The two events were a resounding success with the sell-out crowd of over 10,000 excited guests leaving the venue fired-up to see the movie. With a Japan-centered strategy in place, *Star Wars Episode 1: The Phantom Menace* went on to achieve the highest gross box office of any Star Wars film released to-date in Japan.

And for the Country Manager, showing persistence and resilience won him the trust and confidence of his team.

Raising the profile of Japan in your company's global strategy

There are very sound historical and cultural reasons why Japanese people might tend to show insular attitudes, appearing indifferent or disengaged, or believing that they have been overlooked. Some managers were able to overcome this by convincing the Japan team that being part of a larger strategy was a good thing that could give them an advantage over local competition. They introduced a number of measures to heighten awareness of being part of something larger.

Several contributors talked about how they enlisted the help of their CEO and Head of International to engage Japan in the larger global strategy. They encouraged their head office bosses to visit the Japan office, and also provide video updates, and written messages to the Japan team. In many cases, the Japan subsidiary had disengaged somewhat from head office and perceived of themselves as a small local company. But getting the bigger picture directly from the CEO showed them that they were part of something bigger and also raised the profile of the Japan team in the group's global operations.

Another measure was to bring group companies under one roof. It is quite common for a large global company to have several group companies operating independently in Japan. Frank Foley was involved in such a move when HarperCollins moved in with The Wall Street Journal in Tokyo, which gave a clear signal to employees that they were part of a larger and coherent whole. In another example, the head of a media company provided office space for a Japan-based scout for an American baseball team which was also owned by his parent company. This simple gesture eventually grew into a highly popular sidebar event for the media company's Japanese partners tacked onto an annual trade show in the US.

Communication

Language

As many visitors to Japan will attest, Japan continues to under-perform in English-language ability. Even in companies involved in international business, relatively few employees have what could be called "communicative competence" in English. This skills deficit is widely known, and many companies task their HR departments to provide English language classes or study support. However, it is usually regarded as an employee benefit or perk, and classes are held at awkward times so as not to interfere with the employee's "real work." What's more, HR rarely has knowledge of the subject and does not know how to evaluate providers or services. As a result, programs are allowed to run on with no oversight, and English language competence is seen as somehow peripheral to the company's interests.

We believe this attitude is mistaken. Any company involved in international business should regard competence in English as a core business skill. If an employee needs English language support, whether for a specific job task or over a longer-term, it should be as readily available as technical support or any other internal service.

Soon after taking over the reins at the Japan office of a global publishing house, co-author Frank Foley found that the company's English language classes were poorly attended and there was scant evidence of any progress or achievement. The reasons were not difficult to find. They were too long and were held in the early morning or evening, completely at odds with the needs of a workforce comprised overwhelmingly of women with childcare commitments, and the course content was boring and irrelevant.

He turned to Business English and communications expert (and fellow co-author) David Pinsker to re-think the entire approach. The result was "*eigo kurinikku*" (English Clinic), a drop-in center modeled on an on-site doctor's clinic, where any employee could bring their English "ailment" to the expert for a confidential individual consultation. The "clinic" was open for two hours during normal work hours, and consultations were available in 15-minute units. Instead of using a textbook to define a syllabus, each consultation revolved round a language task or need identified by the employee, such as a presentation, an email response, or preparation for an overseas visitor. Language issues that were addressed in the consultations were then presented to the larger group (and shared with HR) in a monthly wrap-up and report session. With its flexible scheduling, user-generated content and one-on-one "consultation" format, *eigo kurinikku* was able to assist several employees who would not attend traditional English classes. Beyond that, however, the initiative also had a strategic impact. By holding *eigo kurinikku* during the normal workday, and by presenting the language issues from the consultations to the whole group, English competence was brought in from the twilight hours and integrated into the normal business environment of the company. This gave an unambiguous message that the company regarded competence in English as a core business skill.

Cross-cultural communication

Not surprisingly, cross-cultural misunderstanding was a frequent topic in our interviews. Where communication breaks down, it often starts with nothing more than simple misunderstanding arising from the cultural difference in communication styles. Tim Sullivan dates such differences back to the Greek philosophers and the time of Confucius. Western thinking is a legacy of the Greeks which "rightly or wrongly, puts 'truth' at the top of the hierarchy of values. And to get to the truth they invented the dialectic, what most people today call 'debating'." In Japan, the corresponding value is "harmony," which originally came from Confucius. "It's not that the Japanese don't like the truth, but when truth and harmony collide, often the truth gets swept under the rug to preserve harmony. So how do Japanese managers avoid harmony-shattering confrontation? They negotiate behind the scenes to avoid debate at the meeting!"

Sullivan shares a comment from a young American manager who had just heard him speak about the different philosophical legacies. In the manager's own words,

"I was participating in a conference call with Japan. Half the participants were Americans, half were Japanese. We were discussing the testing of a component being developed for a new model. One of the Japanese engineers in Japan, 'Mr. Tanaka,' reported information that was incorrect. I was tempted to speak up, but instead, I whispered to my Japanese boss that I had the correct information from a more recent test. He whispered back that I should not mention it, that he would take care of it offline. At the time, I was confused about why he wouldn't just mention it right there. Thanks to your (Sullivan's) explanation about the Greeks and Confucius, I now understand why my boss behaved the way he did." [45]

Several contributors noted that, on the western side, many people have a tendency to gloss over the challenges in an almost cursory manner and then assume that they have agreement, using phrases like: "Do you get it? Do you understand?" On the

Japanese side there is a culture where detail matters, and where "yes" simply means "I've heard you" and not necessarily "I am agreeing with you." Hearing the Japanese "yes" is enough for many western managers to assume that everything that has been said, and all the underpinning context behind it, was understood and accepted. Without a culturally adept Japan-Insider Country Manager mediating such communications, there is always a risk that a misunderstanding will mutate into a breakdown, or that it will be left undiscovered, a disaster waiting to happen.

In one example:

"HQ was converting the company globally to a single VoIP telephone system. I was actually quite concerned about this because the vendor did not have a presence in Japan, which meant we were the guinea pig, and without local customer support. HQ had anticipated that Japan would be the most difficult market so had left it to last. By the time they came to us, they were insistent that, because they didn't have major problems in other markets, Japan would be OK too. To further heighten my anxiety, my US-based boss told me that I was not to get involved in the project. He said that HQ would pay for an interpreter for the entire project so HQ IT could handle the project directly with my IT team. After two and half decades leading foreign businesses in Japan, I knew this was not going to end well, but I also knew that the best way forward was to let them find that out for themselves. Sure enough, a couple of weeks into the project, my head of IT came to ask my advice on some looming issues to do with restrictions on VoIP services in Japan. He explained that, somehow, HQ had the impression that Japan had accepted the system already and they were ready to move to installation. When I

checked with HQ, it was indeed was a classic "yes doesn't mean yes" misunderstanding. Luckily it was still relatively early in the project, and we were able to address the issues, but it could have been a disaster."

It is important to note that having an interpreter present does not always solve the problem, since the misunderstandings are often cultural as well as linguistic. Although it is advisable to use an interpreter where possible, one of the crucial contributions of Japan-Insider Country Managers is to "read the room" so that any misunderstandings are addressed before they get out of hand.

Sontaku is a noble concept that refuses to be consigned to history. It was the word of the year in 2017 due to a political and financial scandal. The main protagonist used the word to describe his intuition and willingness to carry out his superior's unspoken instructions. It was generally agreed that the word was untranslatable, but it can be understood as an assumption made to save face or earn favor.

It is not a word one would hear often, but the behavior it describes is not uncommon. It explains this example from a contributor working in corporate training of information being filtered by local senior management:

"Something I've always been vigilant of is that senior management often try to apply a filter when working with foreign bosses. They like to control the flow of communication, both up and down... They are not being vindictive. Their reasoning is simply that head office wouldn't understand if we told them the truth, or that the Japanese team won't respond well to the foreign boss's aggressive expectations."

Although possibly honorable in its intention and its samurai pedigree, *sontaku* is the enemy of open and clear communication in any organization.

Head office misunderstanding and preconceptions

There can also be misunderstanding on the head office side. This can range from over-compensating for cultural differences, to being oblivious to them. In an example of over-compensation, one contributor said that while cultural sensitivity is important, it must be put it in context. He said that some international companies coming into Japan take cultural sensitivity so seriously that they "arrive almost wearing kimonos." His advice to such companies is to first "meet the market, have the conversation firstly with the teams that you hire, and then, if there are things that need to be changed, like accommodating a longer sales cycle, etc., then do that as needed."

At the other extreme, one highly experienced Japan-Insider Country Manager was employed by a global communications and marketing agency with a brief to address poorly performing staff at its Japan branch. Upon joining, he discovered that the problem was not a lack of skills but inappropriate allocation of skills to tasks. The core reason was that head office had misread how staff is trained and managed at Japanese companies. In his own words,

"Japanese companies tend to hire at a much more junior (entry) level and then build up the skill and career of employees over decades and across many divisions internally. So, the western company thinks they are hiring a trained brand marketing specialist or brand design specialist from a big Japanese brand

like Kao *or* Lion *but what they are getting is a generalist who had gone from division to division, and who might have been in marketing for just the last two or three years."*

Several contributors talked about the impact of the very different management and training styles used in Japan, and those used in western companies. According to one,

"I remember joining a shipping company as a new recruit nearly 30 years ago. And it was training by osmosis. I was put in the HR division, then the PR division, and then I was put in the operations division, but every time I would be given a task with no instruction how to carry it out - no instruction on who to talk to, where to go for the information on past cases - you were expected to figure it out. And that is, or was, pretty common in Japanese companies that form the standard of Japanese business management. So managers are not good at mentoring – or maybe they mentor but they don't train, task, or evaluate very well by western standards."

Recalling a more recent experience as the incoming Japan Country Manager for a global advertising agency, the same contributor shows that not much has changed in 30 years:

"...many of the local staff didn't understand their roles and priorities. They were aware of the problem, but they didn't know how to fix it - what they should be prioritizing, what they should be working on, what they should be providing. This was because many of them came from other foreign companies and understood what was expected of them working in a western company, but our company was being managed in a very Japanese way... (where) a Japanese boss will give a 'do this!' or 'make this!' sort

of instruction, but will generally not tell their staff how to do it, or exactly what the output should look like, or how they will be judged on it. It's basically 'do this and figure it out!'"

Businesses in the rest of the world are also susceptible to the "othering" of Japan. Sometimes, due to insufficient or inaccurate communication, Japan is seen as too distant and too difficult, and a cautious head office is reluctant to relinquish control to the Country Manager. In cases like this, the "Japan is different" can be a useful cloak to hide inaction and lack of commitment.

One of our contributors, a restless and inquisitive manager in the advertising industry, took on a portfolio of successful international clients whose campaigns failed so often in Japan that they were almost resigned to under-performance. He refused to accept "Japan is different" as an explanation. He discovered that the global programs were in fact programs that had been developed in the US or the UK, and that was where the problem lay. He took it upon himself to educate his clients' global teams, arranging half-day workshops for their global CEO and heads of communications, advertising and marketing, which would explain the Japanese consumer's viewpoint and brand expectations. He would show his clients what their Japanese competitors were doing in marketing and branding, and put the question to them: "What does this brand mean? What does it offer?" It was a question they could not answer at the time, but it was the starting point for defining a real Japan strategy. As he tells the story,

"That allowed us to do two things with the client. Firstly, it allowed us to tailor the global communications to be relevant for

the Japanese market, and secondly it enabled us to do something that was forbidden globally, and that was to develop independent "for-the-market" communications on a local budget, which their local people in Japan had always wanted to do. The net result was that we were able to grow our business with them."

Two critical relationships

One of the most important roles of Japan-Insider Country Managers is being the intermediary between their parent/regional company and the local operation. To succeed, it is critical that they have excellent relationships with two key people: their head office-based boss, and their local 2IC.

The boss/head office relationship

We believe that a study of the appointment and training of head office-based International Heads is worthy of a book in itself. It takes a special type of manager. Not only do you have to understand, or at least be sensitive to, the cultural challenges across multiple markets, you also must be a great manager of senior managers - people who, in their own market, are seen by partners and staff as being the local CEO.

Having a good working relationship with one's boss is important for any manager in any context, but it is absolutely critical for Country Managers. Unlike head-office and head office-adjacent colleagues, Country Managers often lack formal and informal support and protection, cut off from access to the CEO, mentors, head office networks and HR support. They are at the wrong end of proximity bias. Furthermore, contracts at senior or director level may not have the stringent protection offered by Japan's laws against summary dismissal, leaving foreign Country Managers dangerously exposed.

Japan-Insider Country Managers interviewed for this study had a wide range of experiences in terms of their relationship with their head office-based boss. At one extreme, many contributors were able to share positive stories about supportive and internationally savvy bosses. We have included several such stories in the words of the contributors themselves in Part Two of this book. But there were also stories of communication and trust breakdown which, in one case, resulted in the Country Manager not having their contract renewed. The reputational damage can potentially ruin a career in which Country Managers have invested decades, during which irreplaceable business relationships have been built.

So, why do problems arise? In some cases, it was simply a communication issue, or a head office misunderstanding of the roles and training in Japan. Frank Foley shared a story of when he took over Thomas and Friends Japan. Head office were complaining that Japan didn't have a strategy and pushed back on any ideas from outside Japan. When he talked to the local team, he found exactly the opposite. The local 2IC and his team - and their licensing partners - were brimming with terrific ideas for the brand, but just weren't presenting their case well. In this case, the solution was as easy as resolving the communication problem. The result was a highly effective local strategy for Japan with many of the initiatives being adopted by other international markets too.

Another contributor talked about his boss accusing him of identifying too closely with the host country. This is a scenario mentioned by several contributors in which the Japan-Insider Country Manager has inherited disgruntled staff and/or Japanese partners. The Japanese side is likely to welcome the appointment of somebody "who understands Japan" and who can explain the Japanese position back to head office. The Country Manager is pulled into a mediator role, or worse, into being co-opted as a spokesperson for the Japan side. When that happens, Country Managers can lose the support of head office, and might be written off with the anachronistic and racist epithet of having "gone native." Unfortunately, there is no compensatory benefit from the Japan side when this happens, so even if the manager stays in the position, his or her influence is undermined.

In another example from the character and brand-licensing business, the challenge was due to a change in ownership. The company had just been bought by a private equity firm. The new owner wanted to conduct an audit of its master licensee in Japan - one of the largest and most respected firms in the business, with an excellent track record. The Japan-Insider Country Manager was more than willing to help facilitate the audit, but the new owners insisted that it be conducted directly between head office and the master licensee with minimal involvement from the local team. By treating the Country Manager and his local team with suspicion, in one fell swoop they succeeded in seriously compromising hard-earned trust with the master licensee, and in alienating the Country Manager.

There were also examples of bad bosses. The most common symptoms were micromanagement and disregard for the local hierarchy and relationships in Japan by the Head of International. Examples included the Head of International quizzing staff members about the Country Manager's performance, arranging calls and meetings with Japanese partners without involving the Country Manager, and blocking mission-critical decisions advocated by the Country Manager.

In the words of one contributor,

"The Head of International must understand that when employing a Country Manager, they are dealing with someone who has spent many years building a reputation in their market.

If you screw up as their boss, you are causing serious damage to that person's reputation on their home ground. That's quite a heavy responsibility."

At the request of contributors, we have not shared their specific stories regarding issues with bosses and head office, but we would like to highlight that having robust processes connecting the Country Manager with head office is critical to mitigating risks for both parties. This includes everything from search and selection, on-boarding, ongoing training, communication, and conflict resolution. For the company, a poor decision is potentially very costly, not only financially but also in terms of damaged relationships and loss of trust with Japanese partners and customers. From the Country Manager's perspective, selecting the right company, and performing well is even more critical. Failure, or even the perception of failure, could be a career-ending catastrophe.

The issue of "re-training" when there are significant changes to the job description, deserves special attention. One example we heard was of a Japan-Insider Country Manager being a victim of his own success. A Japan-Insider was originally employed for a business development role for the Japan launch by a global company. The person did a terrific job and the business launched and grew quickly. With the right re-training the individual expected to step into the operational leadership position, but in the absence of a re-training process the company moved him on and appointed someone else.

Rather than looking at the on-boarding process and training of Country Managers in isolation, international companies would be well-advised to consider ongoing training and support for Heads of International together with the Country Manager. From the manager's perspective, asking "what if…?" may not seem like a good question when interviewing for a Country Manager position, but it would be wise to ensure that the company has a robust conflict resolution process which will be available to them in the worst-case scenario.

The 2IC relationship

And finally, possibly the most important relationship for successful Japan-Insider Country Managers - that with their 2IC. As one contributor put it, "I have been most effective and enjoyed the greatest success when I worked well with a terrific Japanese 2IC. Conversely, I have struggled - and failed spectacularly on one occasion - whenever that relationship broke down."

In many respects, the secret of a great Country Manager/2IC relationship in a cross-cultural context is the same as for a domestic company in any country. It is based on mutual trust, complementary skills, excellent two-way communication, and a clear delineation of roles. A subtle but important difference in the case of Japan country management, however, is in the definition of those respective roles. And the biggest problems arise when roles are inappropriately defined.

In an American company for example, the distinction in roles is often described in terms of "strategy" which is led by the CEO, and "operations" which falls under the 2IC. The CEO is focused more ON the business, while the 2IC is focused IN the business. There is a clear element of hierarchy, with the 2IC's primary role being to free up space for the CEO to concentrate on growing the business. [46] That is not to imply that the 2IC is a simply a "yes man." On the contrary, he/she is also responsible for pushing back when appropriate on "how" to proceed, while remaining loyal and supportive of the CEO's vision of what the company is trying to achieve. But ultimately the buck stops with the CEO and a good 2IC knows when debate ends and to implement like it was their own decision. [47]

A point made by several contributors is that in a Japanese cross-cultural situation, the respective roles of the non-Japanese Country Manager and their local 2IC are better defined in terms of "head office-focus" vs "local-focus", rather than a hierarchical distinction between strategy and operations. In fact, most contributors stressed the importance of close collaboration with the local 2IC on both strategy and operations. Neither person alone has all the necessary skills and experience, but the two people combined represent a powerful force that can give the company a significant advantage.

The non-Japanese Country Manager should have a deeper understanding of head office's larger strategy, its expectations of Japan, and the head office resources that Japan can draw on. The local 2IC will bring a deeper knowledge and insights on the Japanese market. They both know enough about the other's area to work effectively together in the middle, communicating on progress and challenges, fine-tuning plans (head office and local), new business development, staff development and the like. While the buck must ultimately stop with the Country Manager, the relationship is more an equal partnership than an explicit hierarchy typical in western companies.

One contributor referred to this as "two-in-a box."

"Whether it's the foreigner as the Country Manager and the Japanese as No. 2, or the other way around, it doesn't matter. The important thing is that they are aligned and working well together. There will be crossover where both people will be effective, but the foreigner's primary role is to manage head office, and the Japanese person's role is to be deep into the local business. It's got to be a team effort, including the head office-based Head of International. If any one of these players is not there, the magic won't work!"

Several contributors added that it is also critical that your Japanese staff believe in and trust the Country Manager /2IC partnership. Any hint of discord at the top could spell disaster for your organization.

What we've learned

As we noted in the Preface, the inspiration for this book came from the discovery of a diverse range of top-class Japan-Insider Country Managers speaking on social media during Covid. We dubbed it our "Covid silver lining." Now, having spoken directly with some of the best of these managers for this book, we think that silver-lining is, if anything, an understatement. There are nuggets of gold in what these people have to say.

We invite you to read their stories in their own words in Part Two.

- PART TWO -

THE INTERVIEWS

1
- Derek Baines -

"Sometimes proposals from Japan appear either bizarre or boring from the perspective of a non-Japan person."

Profile

Derek Baines learned Japanese language in high school in Brisbane, Australia and majored in Japanese and Asian Studies at Griffith University. He has been working in the international business field for over 35 years including senior roles with C. Itoh, two World Expositions, Qantas Airways and Tourism Australia. He is the author of two collections of poetry and a novel, set in World War II Japan and post-war Australia.

Frank's Foreword

When he arrived in Tokyo in the midst of the Covid pandemic, after an extended period waiting for a work visa for Japan, Derek Baines inherited a highly experienced team who, for reasons not of their own making, had not had a senior leader on the ground for some time. I was interested in how he dealt with the challenge of reestablishing the relationship with head office, and what Japan-insider skills were important in achieving this.

Interview

FRANK: You have a very interesting job representing Tourism Australia in Japan. There must have been a lot of competition during the hiring process. What do you think you offered that the other candidates could not?

DEREK: I think it was the combination of my industry expertise and Japanese language/culture skills. Many people have one or the other, but, in my industry, to have both is rare. The very fact that you can speak Japanese well puts other stakeholders at ease. It opens doors, and it opens minds to possibilities. And over time you get to understand the nuances and cultural insights, and develop the ability to read between the lines.

Language and my long association with Japan enabled me to draw upon old relationships with people who, over the years, have become quite influential. Our business is essentially marketing, so access to influencers is very important. For example, when we were looking at how to increase our profile in the entertainment business, I rekindled a relationship with a now very famous Japanese actor, from a famous family of actors. We had worked together years ago in Australia way back in 1981 when she was making a documentary. This is not something that someone new to Japan without any experience could conceive of doing.

It's important for the Country Manager to have a certain number of direct relationships. It gives head office the reassurance that the Japan office is in good hands, so they don't micromanage too much. And it also shows my local team that "this guy knows Japan." It legitimizes you as somebody who can fit in, and does fit in. It shows that you are not somebody they have to spend time looking after, and that you can help them in their jobs and add value.

Having perspective as a Japan-savvy foreigner also helps you stand out with Japanese industry partners. For example, my PR team knew I was an author in my spare time, and they came up with the idea of me writing a series of articles for a trade magazine. They pitched it to one of the biggest Japanese online travel magazines, and they loved the idea and asked me to write a series of four articles. Personally, I've always wanted to write Japanese at a better level, and this project spurred me on to do that. But more importantly, professionally it showed that there was interest in the industry in hearing what the Japan-Insider foreigner had to say about Japan and tourism. I don't think any of the trade publications have ever gone down this path. They've published content that we give them, but that's maybe about a competition or video/still photography about a destination; but as an opinion piece, from a personal perspective, this is a new area. We can have umpteen Japanese journalists and influencers writing about Australia – and that's great and we want that – but "what does this guy think? He speaks and writes in Japanese!" I think it's an important part of my role, and well spotted by my PR team.

FRANK: It shows that Marshall McLuhan was right: the medium is the message! The fact that the Japan-Insider Country Manager is telling the story is the point.

DEREK: At the beginning I was a bit reluctant. Although I like writing, I wondered if I might be perceived as self-aggrandizing, but people said there was great interest in my take on things.

FRANK: Is this something you would encourage other companies to try, use their Japan-Insider Country Manager almost like talent?

DEREK: Yes, I think there is a growing appetite for engaging opinion pieces by Japan-insiders like us, especially in this era of digital marketing when you often need to do something different to stand out. And it was also a great exercise for me in terms of crystallizing my thinking.

FRANK: So, what about your local team?

DEREK: I had only met one of my team before I started in the role, so I'm sure they were thinking, "Is this guy going to work? Is he going to be demanding? Or is he going to be helping us do what we do?" My intention is to be as helpful as possible, to support them and make the team successful. I know that a previous occupant of this role saw himself as a figurehead, and didn't add a lot of value, didn't have good relations with the team, and didn't respect their roles.

FRANK: From their perspective, besides your local contacts and PR talent, what other value do you add?

DEREK: A big part of what I do is advocating a position to head office. My team are actually very good at presenting opportunities and challenges, but it also carries a lot of weight if I advocate for them. I also find that, sometimes, it takes a person with a foot in both camps to get the idea across to people at head office. That's not to say that we would always succeed or get what we want, but I'd say that in nine times out of 10, I can crystallize their requests or opinions into something that will have impact at the decision-making level.

FRANK: Do you have any examples?

DEREK: Sometimes proposals from Japan appear either bizarre or boring from the perspective of a non-Japan person. For example, we've done a lot of webinars and seminars with some of the travel media which border on the nerdy or academic from a western context, but really worked well here. In an example of something that was seen as a little bizarre, we were doing a campaign with a beautifully shot 8D video series which had an immersive sound feature. It was the first time a tourist organization had used this technology. One big question was what paid media we would use in Japan. The Japan side, including our advertising agency wanted to use Spotify because of the sound-based experience. People in head office were very skeptical about focusing on an audio channel for this high-end video content. The team asked me to help convince my boss, which I did, and we did advertise on Spotify Japan's free website. It turned out our instincts were right, and Spotify was one the best performing promotion channels for us on that campaign.

And an example of something seeming simply boring was where we designed a competition with one of the travel magazines where people would actually pay the magazine ¥5,000 to participate. They were put in groups with people they didn't know and were tasked to design new Australia tour packages. So, people were giving up their time and paying to design a tour package which they probably would never get to enjoy! Head office's reaction was "why would anybody even do that!" But again, our Japanese team's instinct was spot on, and the campaign was a huge success. People really got into it. And it was entirely self-funding through the fee paid to the magazine. We got a big "good on you" from head office on that one!

FRANK: You've reminded me of a campaign we did with Harlequin Romance to find Japan's Mr. Harlequin. It was a social media driven competition. The main talent we got to host events was Haruna Ai, Japan's first winner of the "Miss International Queen" transgender beauty pageant in 2009. She is hugely popular in Japan with a big social media following, and a regular on TV panel shows and the like. I remember it did raise some eyebrows in the US, but it was a very successful campaign that made total sense in the Japanese context.

How would you describe your team's relationship with head office?

DEREK: They have a very good understanding of the big picture because most of them have worked for Tourism Australia much longer than I have. They've had years of conditioning on how things work, what problems arise, and who is doing what. However, I sometimes do need to mediate in a more specific sense, in explaining particular situations and circumstances. I'm also able to give them advanced warning if something is about to change that they might not otherwise get. I am very conscious of my role as a "stabilizer", which you can only do if you have a foot in both camps.

FRANK: How would you describe your own relationship with head office?

DEREK: The first thing is that I am blessed with a terrific boss. He was the one who encouraged me to apply for the position and he advocated strongly on my behalf. He knows the Japanese market very well and he believed that I was the best person. There was actually a degree of trepidation among other senior head office people because of a bad experience with a previous appointment to the position. Without my boss's support, I'm not sure that I would have got the job, and I am very grateful for that. Now, I think I have won the trust and support of the head office leadership team. I am listened to, and I think respected.

With head office it's all about leveraging the strengths on each side, respecting the roles, respecting the people, not having a completely one-way tracking of the relationship. You want the right balance between local autonomy and the overall corporate strategy. In my current organization, I feel that is understood and respected on both sides. There are things that our head office clearly leaves to our regional offices, especially on the detail of marketing. On the other hand, the over-arching brand strategy is an area where we respect and follow head office's direction. Those dynamics are embodied in the personal relationships that we all have throughout the organization; and even to our stakeholders beyond, such as tourism operators and state government offices. And it's critical that we all continue to listen and communicate in the current environment as tourism recovers post-Covid.

2
- Elmar Bob -

"This was definitely a case where only a foreigner could get the desired result. You might call it 'using the gaijin card!'"

Profile

Born in Germany and educated in the US from the age of 15, Elmar Bob came to Japan in the 1990s to join an all-Japanese sales team dealing exclusively with domestic clients. He later moved to the fashion industry, first with French luxury goods maker LVMH where he headed Kenzo KK, and then Yves Saint Laurent KK as General Manager. In 1999, Bob returned to Germany to set up operations for, and eventually take public, the UK-based Matchnet, PLC. In 2007, he accepted a new challenge with the German behemoth Siemens in their Mexico office. Siemens brought him back to Japan in 2009, as Head of Supply Chain Management and Business Development. Bob later moved to the Japan office of enterprise application software giant SAP, where he headed one of their cloud companies named Ariba. He is currently Country Manager for a Japanese/American IT enterprise.

Frank's Foreword

Elmar Bob believes that it's important for non-Japanese Country Managers to be prepared to play the *gaijin* (foreigner) card, and sometimes to be the "bad cop" in negotiations if justified by the situation. In our interview, he was able to share some colorful, and sometimes emotional, stories about how being the *gaijin* boss enabled him to achieve a result that would have been very difficult, if not impossible, for a Japanese boss.

Interview

FRANK: One of the big questions for a company setting up in Japan is whether they should hire a foreigner or a Japanese person for the country management role. Can you tell me about some times where you've done something that a Japanese person in that position might not have been able to do?

ELMAR: Let me give you one example which was particularly significant for me. I was Head of Supply Chain at Siemens Japan at the time of the March 2011 Tohoku earthquake. We were being bombarded with calls from hospitals to replace sensitive machinery that had been damaged by the quake. Of course, we agreed to do so, and at no payment, but we had a lot of logistical challenges. We knew we had some spare capacity in China which could be supplied faster than going back to Germany, but Japanese customs was refusing to let them in. My team had tried everything, but the customs guy just wouldn't budge. This was literally a case of life or death, so we had to do something!

I talked to my team and we decided on a "good cop, bad cop" strategy. They had already tried the good cop approach, so my job was to be the bad cop. I went to confront the customs people myself. When I asked why they couldn't let the machines in, they said that my company was authorized to import from Germany only, and that Japan had restrictions on imports from China. I explained that the machines in China were exactly the same as the ones in Germany, and that so many Japanese hospitals needed them urgently. We had a long discussion, but they refused to budge. In the end I said, "OK, I understand," and I pulled out my cell phone and went to take a photo of the customs official. "No, no," he objected, "no pictures!" So, I said to him, "I'm taking this picture to show the mothers and fathers of Fukushima the face of the person who is responsible for not letting in these machines." He said "OK. Wait. Let me talk to my boss." And in 30 minutes the machines had cleared customs.

The challenges didn't end there. Truck drivers were in short supply so, to make sure the machines got to hospitals as quickly as possible, I ended up driving the truck up to Fukushima myself with my team in tow. Before we left Tokyo we bought lots of toys and things for the kids which they appreciated a lot. It was one of the most significant things I've done in my life.

Not that it was my goal, but because of that incident, the hospitals in the region only wanted to deal with me, because I was the guy that actually helped them. We were able to act quickly despite the bureaucratic challenges which is not easy in Japan. It felt good to be able to help. This was definitely a case where only a foreigner could get the desired result. You might call it "using the *gaijin* card"!

As an aside, when we got to Fukushima, the Red Cross and the US military were already there, but the Japanese military wasn't there yet. So, the *gaijin* were the first responders to this Japanese problem.

FRANK: I've used that "good cop, bad cop" strategy myself with my Japanese colleague. We would agree our roles before we went into a negotiation. Sometimes that's what's needed to get the desired outcome.

ELMAR: And sometimes you need to threaten to publicly name and shame people!

In another case, I was trying to reach the CEO of a well-known Japanese company to talk about one of our products. Our sales team said this guy is booked out for the next six months, which they read as "he doesn't want to talk to us." But I didn't want to give up and thought again about how to use the *gaijin* card. I knew where he was working, and I knew that he was an early bird. I bought donuts, and waited in the lobby from around 06:30, just minding my own business. For three days nothing happened, but on the fourth day he appeared and asked me, "Are you the person that's always waiting for me?" I said "Yes," and he asked what I wanted. I said, "Five minutes of your time with coffee and donuts, and then I'm gone." We got to talking, and five minutes turned into an hour, and we actually sold him some of our SAP software.

Again, I think this is a tactic that only a foreigner could get away with. When I told my team I was going to do it, they said it would never work. But I knew that many Japanese people – even very high-ranking managers – make allowances for foreigners that they would never do for local staff. Of course, we also face some challenges as foreigners, but this was one of those cases where being a foreigner actually helped.

Another role as the Japan-insider foreigner was to identify new opportunities in the market, especially ones that leverage your parent company's global strengths. After Fukushima, and when I was still with Siemens, the government put in place a massive alternative energy plan to create a lot of mega solar farms. We were the top energy company in Europe, maybe in the world, with a long track record in Japan in building this kind of power plant. At that time, Siemens Japan was about 85% healthcare, 13% industry and maybe 2% energy. I pitched to senior management in Japan that we beef up the alternative energy division here with new hires and really go after that market. Siemens Japan had about 2,000 people, with maybe 20 in the energy division. I wanted to increase that to about 100 people, but even 50 would have been fine. Japan is a big territory for Siemens and there were incredible subsidies for solar plants right after 2011. There was no question in my mind that it was a lucrative business. It was based on "Feed-In-Tariffs" (FIT), meaning you are paid for feeding power into the grid. The FIT was four times higher than what was being paid in Europe. Even after it was halved in subsequent years, it was still double the rate in Europe!

I was selling the idea to the president of the Japan operation. As Head of Supply Chain, I was part of the senior leadership team at the top level but unfortunately wasn't able to convince them. Their reasoning was that they thought the risk of failure outweighed any potential upside. While I understood where they were coming from in the context of Japanese business culture, their lack of any sort of entrepreneurial spirit saddened me because Siemens is supposed to be a great entrepreneurial engineering company. One of the reasons Siemens is not doing that well in Japan is because the business culture is so risk averse and not really interested in trying new ideas.

This incident led me to quit Siemens, and to start a solar company in Japan with the help of a German firm. We did this for two years. We did quite well as an early mover, but after a while, Chinese and domestic competition came in and the market became tough for smaller players like us.

Comparing when I first came to Japan to now, I have to ask, "where have all the entrepreneurs gone?" There was Walkman, there was *tamagochi*; there were cool innovative brands like Olympus and Canon. Now, what's cool and innovative about Japan? Nobody takes risks anymore!

FRANK: So, can you tell me more about your career after Siemens and the solar power partnership?

ELMAR: I joined SAP, which is an IT company and the largest company in Germany by market cap. In Japan, SAP had about 1,500 people. The business culture was similar to Siemens - locally run and quite conservative. I was running a division of SAP that dealt with a lot of Japanese bankers, who themselves are renowned for being very risk-averse, conservative people. But one day they said to me, "Elmar, there's a new technology out there called the Blockchain, and there's a payment system based on it called XRP Ripple. Maybe you guys should look into it!" This was still early days for Blockchain and the more I read about it, the more I was amazed. So, I pitched it to our local SAP Japan management team many times, but just got a flat "No way!" I then suggested we partner in it, but still got a resounding "No!" All three major Japanese banks are now invested in Blockchain, so SAP Japan was being even more conservative than the banks!

FRANK: Would you say that the decision of whether to appoint a non-Japanese or a Japanese national as Country Manager comes down to the nature of your business? If you are in a conservative business that is slow-moving, and it's all about getting on well with your Japanese partners, then probably a Japanese old hand is the best person for the company?

ELMAR: I think the big difference between Japanese and western business culture is openness to other perspectives and ideas. In a German company, for example, it is no longer unusual to have a leader from France or England, or America. Race, gender, sexual orientation are irrelevant. This didn't happen overnight and there was a learning process, but nowadays it's not unusual to have a very diverse group of people running companies. And I think that makes them better and stronger. Japan has not learned this yet.

There are many experienced Japanese-speaking foreigners in Japan who could offer fresh perspectives and ideas, but they are massively under-utilized. Sure, we might not all speak perfect Japanese or act in a perfect Japanese manner, but that's a good thing. More diversity and more new thinking are good things!

Sports is one of the few areas where this has been happening for many years, and to great effect. The Japanese rugby team couldn't survive without foreigner players. J-League soccer is the same. They have an influence because the clubs know that without those foreigners, they are not going to be successful. The same thing will happen in business.

FRANK: Do you have any examples of where you succeeded in changing the culture, or a mindset, at your company?

ELMAR: When we had foreign executives come to Siemens or SAP, we would have to prepare one-page briefing documents on key deals - who? where? what? why? Inevitably the reaction from my team would be, "I've got so many deals; how am I going to fit them on one page?" In the Japanese world, if you haven't written every single thing on the document, you haven't done it correctly. I would point out that it was called a *briefing* document because it should present the needle-changing deals in a 15~20 minute read for the senior executive. Even then, they would come back with four pages. I would reject it time and again. After about three months they came up with a one-pager, which still needed some improvement, but was still huge progress. It took time to change their way of thinking, but they did learn, and they got better at it and are still doing it.

I think this reflects something very fundamental in Japanese culture. I see it a lot in daily life in Japan - that people spend a lot of time on meaningless tasks, things that I would never waste time on. And I see Japanese have a hard time prioritizing things. You see that sometimes when disasters happen. They don't know what's more important because everything's important.

FRANK: Finally, how do you think Japanese companies could use us "Japan-insiders"?

ELMAR: I have never once had a Japanese recruiter reach out to me, even though I have spent most of my career in Japan. Why not? I should be a natural target. Any Japanese company that has regular dealings with or maybe even owns foreign companies should be leveraging people like us. It requires different negotiation skills to what they are used to - like how to say "no", or how to present a counterargument to a price that's too high.

I don't know if this due to fear of sharing information or pride or shame in asking a foreigner to do it. But as a businessperson I know that if I can't negotiate with a Chinese company, I would bring in another Chinese person to do the negotiation. And I wouldn't have an issue about it. So why can't Japanese companies do that with us?

3

- Geoffrey Bossiere -

"You have to treat Japan as an entity unto itself and remake yourself accordingly."

Profile

Geoffrey Bossiere began his career in Japan in 1986, very much in the *genba*. First working as a waiter in upmarket Ginza's Suehiro restaurant, and later as a door-to-door salesperson for a temporary staffing services agency, he quickly learned Japanese while also honing his cross-cultural communication skills. Geoffrey was then employed at Dainana Securities in Tokyo where he became a licensed securities trader.

Dainana's investment in a movie production company initiated his 30+ year relationship with Hollywood, beginning in 1992 at 20th Century Fox International as a financial analyst. In 1993, after completing an MBA at UCLA, Fox moved Geoffrey back to Japan where he quickly rose through the ranks. In 1996 he was promoted to General Manager of the Japan operation and established the company as a market-leading film distributor. In 2001 Geoffrey joined Hollywood-based Revolution Studios as Head of International Distribution. Always at the forefront of entertainment and digital streaming in Japan, he launched his own consultancy company, Shining Prince Entertainment, advising major entertainment brands such as DreamWorks, Paramount Pictures, and IMAX. Later, after leading Hulu's launch in Japan as launch Managing Director, he also advised Netflix and HBO Max. Since 2022 Geoffrey has been developing feature films and television series for the worldwide market.

Frank's Foreword

I first got to know Geoff in the late 1990s. He was Japan Country Manager of 20th Century Fox (Theatrical), and I was running Fox's cable and satellite company in Japan. It was a golden era for the company in Japan, with massive hit movies such as *Titanic*, *Star Wars*, and *Independence Day (ID4)*. The stakes were high, as was the pressure on Geoff. His success in managing relationships - from the larger-than-life personalities in Hollywood, to external Japanese partners and to his own team - had always impressed me. I was keen to hear what he had learned from those experiences in terms of effective Japan Country Management. Also, in addition to being highly creative, Geoff is also an expert in the digital streaming business. Japan is notoriously slow to adapt new technologies and I was interested in Geoff's perspective on that front too.

Interview

FRANK: You have worked for over 30 years in Hollywood filmed entertainment distribution, and more recently in the digital streaming world. What, for you, are the most important things for foreign companies to understand in order to succeed in Japan?

GEOFFREY: Japan is a very competitive market, and to succeed, your strategy must be anchored in these three critical principles. First, it should be long-term. The rule of thumb in Japan is that most things take 2~3 times as long as anywhere else. It's best to be prepared for the long haul. Second, your strategy should leverage your global scale or strengths you may have in other markets, but be tailored for Japanese consumers. As with any major market, and especially one with a very different culture from most, Japan has its idiosyncrasies and it demands its own strategy. Finally, your strategy should be bold and question conventional wisdom whenever appropriate.

FRANK: OK, let's look at each one of these. First, commit to a long-term strategy. Can you give us some examples of what you mean by that?

GEOFFREY: My experience at Fox taught me that to succeed in Japan you must commit to a long-term strategy, and it is critical for your head office executives to have trust and faith in their local leadership team who know the market and are driving that strategy. Overnight success is extremely rare. It takes a persistence and commitment at the very senior levels to have any hope of success because the process is usually time consuming and it's easy to lose focus.

A good example of this is Hulu's initial foray into Japan. When we launched the new service, the owners - Fox and Disney (NBC Universal was a non-voting owner) - had not really bought into a long-term strategy which required more and more investment. In their defense, I admit that Hulu was ahead of its time, given how long it took for streaming services to take off in Japan, and the first mover often has a huge cost burden to pave the way. But I also know the personalities involved and that the real problem was that they had lost sight of the long term. They considered Japan a prickly and difficult market and just didn't see the point of persevering. If they had stayed the course and not sold the Japan operation to Nippon Television (NTV), they would have been in a much stronger position today. They had a first-mover advantage over Netflix by four years and could have cemented their brand here with a much broader, international network. But they didn't follow that route. They sold it off, which was very unfortunate. Disney acquired Fox and ended up launching its own new service, Disney+, from scratch on the same worldwide basis that Hulu should have done many years before.

Hulu had the opportunity to be the first foreign commercial streaming service to have a direct-to-consumer relationship in Japan. It meant no longer having to go through rental shops or theaters or broadcasters, it was the first international direct-to-consumer platform of its kind in Japan. Compared to a time when the film studios used to pay 40~60% of the gross revenue to these intermediaries to distribute their product, this was the first and most direct way of owning the customer and collecting 100% of the revenue, not to mention building very valuable consumer analytics to more efficiently improve customer engagement and market the product. I could see at the time that this was the future of the business, but they didn't have the stomach for it, and perhaps part of the reason was that they were a long way from a truly worldwide launch strategy.

Although the best business model for streaming services has yet to be determined, Disney is perhaps the only one of the traditional studios that believes in "exclusivity", and they have really gone all-in with a long-term and worldwide strategy. They realized early on that huge ancillary revenues coming from Netflix were akin to being addicted to heroin, and they needed to keep their own best product to prevent companies like Netflix from becoming too dominant. They decided some years ago to stop selling to Netflix, and to keep their own content exclusive to their own platform.

Warner Bros Discovery and its new streaming service known as Max (formerly HBO Max) will have to make a decision pretty soon about exclusivity. Currently they are still reliant on the revenues from Netflix and many others. If they take a leaf from Disney's playbook to stick to a long-term strategy and control their intellectual property, this could have a positive impact on their success in Japan. If you want to see *The Matrix*, the *Harry Potter* series or *Game Of Thrones* or *Sex And The City*, the only place to see it should be MAX. But the jury is still out on this in terms of reaching the widest possible audience with the highest potential revenue over the long term.

I think what underlies this is the belief that to succeed in Japan, you must have a Japanese partner. It is an old adage that for decades Japanese business people have been telling foreign executives who want to enter Japan. Of course, it can be true in some instances, especially if the foreign company lacks the resources to go it alone. But what happens with a lot of these companies is in the long run they are swallowed up by the Japanese culture and by their local partner. Trading companies are renowned for engineering these situations.

The important thing is having a long-term focus. Brands like Amazon, Starbucks and Netflix all took a long-term view and were able to go it alone with no partners. These companies hired smart people, took the long view and integrated well with the local industry. Netflix started by working with big talent agencies like Yoshimoto Kogyo and with Fuji TV on co-productions. Netflix are now so dominant that, essentially, all producers work with them. I think it was a smart way of hitting the ground running. Now Netflix is able to develop on their own content with their own production team, working with a vast array of local producers. They are able to compete extremely well for customers because they have both 1) an international production pipeline from around the world, and 2) a proven track record of making local productions from Japan. Some of these have become worldwide hits. They are able to do deals locally while being backed up by a worldwide network. So it's about sticking to a long-term plan and doing good deals, not joint venture partnerships.

Many companies get freaked out and they think, "Oh, we're not going to be able to make it in this market. It's too expensive, it's too difficult, we don't understand it!" But if you take a long-term approach, establish yourself as a local player, and make smart decisions, you can succeed. At the end of the day, you have to treat Japan as an entity unto itself and remake yourself accordingly (and repeatedly). You can't just make superficial changes to your global strategy and expect it to work in Japan. You must have a fit-for-purpose Japan strategy, and stick to it long-term.

FRANK: Your second point was about building a local strategy that leverages global strengths. What examples can you give us there?

GEOFFREY: Lucasfilm had a worldwide campaign for *Star Wars Episode 1: The Phantom Menace*, and were being very careful about how it was coordinated. It was the first new installment in the franchise since the original trilogy from many years earlier and, understandably, Lucasfilm had very specific criteria about how the worldwide campaign should be coordinated. At Fox Japan at the time, we were dealing not only with our own head office in LA, as we would on a normal movie, but also directly with the notoriously uncompromising Lucasfilm. The challenge was compounded by the fact that Lucasfilm had recently hired a non-industry marketing person who had strong ideas of his own.

On the Japan side, we had a strong track record of success with the original trilogy. In Japan alone, those three films combined earned over $200 million. Based on that experience, we had a Japan-specific plan that we were confident would work. We knew we had the opportunity to reach new audience quadrants and that it would require tailored techniques. For example, there was massive latent interest among females who could potentially be drawn in by the amazing costumes and fashion in the new film. We had all this artwork to target fashion magazines and the like. There was this whole strategy with the TV spots and trailers which were called "tone poems", because each had a targeted tone. These were supposed to convey to each of the quadrants a specific feeling or tone of what the film is all about or what could follow.

We adapted these tactics for the Japan market, and some of our tactics drew scrutiny from our LA head office and Lucasfilm's new head of marketing, who had come from the advertising world where he managed accounts like Nike, Apple and Microsoft, and he had been specifically hired by Lucasfilm to bring something special to the new *Star Wars* film. There was interest, but also some pushback. We needed to engage and excite the core fans and create word-of-mouth publicity, but we didn't have a film to screen (due to Lucasfilm's policy).

One of the events that we had proposed was a two-session fan event in the 5,000-seat Tokyo International Forum. We were going to invite cast members, the producer, and special Japanese celebrity guests. Specifically, we invited the actor who played the character of Darth Maul who was also a martial arts expert, and he was going to do some performances and to be interviewed by the producer on stage. Our head office and Lucasfilm thought it was a terrible idea because they worried it would leave the audience unsatisfied.

But we knew Japanese culture and the emphasis on form, presentation and tradition – much like many variety shows on Japanese television. In the US, too much ceremony is too much pomp. But in Japan, it is very common and widely accepted by the general public. A great example of this would be a ceremony that was held recently for the legions of Tokyo Olympics and Paralympics volunteers who were honored in a series of formal events. I don't know if there'd be such a thing in any other country, certainly not in the US. One might throw a party, I suppose, but it'd be much less likely to arrange a formal ceremony that brought all these people together and solemnly thank them all for their service.

So, when it came to releasing the first all new *Star Wars* movie in 16 years, we had a responsibility to the fans to treat it with the respect it deserved. We had to pay attention to detail, right down to the visuals we would show on the screen. Everything had weight, even though from a western perspective it looked more like a publicity stunt.

Just knowing all this, how things are done here, and trusting in that process was what underpinned our success with the Star Wars Japan strategy.

This speaks to the fact that big brand companies often try to impose global strategies without considering the important differences between markets. In our case, Fox's head office were especially concerned about the impact on their relationship with Lucasfilm if the Japan plan failed. It was made harder because when I first described the plan, it didn't sound to them like there was a huge amount of substance. Initially they were dead set against it, saying it was lightweight and would fall on its face.

For *Phantom Menace*, we fought hard and argued we would make it a success. We carried off the two events with great fanfare. We had over 10,000 guests who left satisfied and excited to see the film. In the end, *Star Wars Episode 1: The Phantom Menace*, which was probably the lowest-ranked film in the series in terms of viewer satisfaction, achieved the highest gross box office of any Star Wars film released to-date in Japan, at ¥12.7 billion (about US$115 million at the prevailing exchange rate).

It was based on being in-market, being familiar with the culture, and able to convince a control-oriented head office that a local approach was needed. This victory won us a degree of trust from our head office. It wasn't that we had *carte blanche* to do whatever we wanted after that - we still had to get approval for each marketing campaign - but I would say we provided clarity for the first time in years, giving head office a view on the reality of the Japanese market. It also allowed me, as the General Manager, to win the trust of the team in my ability to fight for what we believed in and win big.

FRANK: Your third point, "Beware of conventional wisdom," is very interesting. Tell us what you mean there.

GEOFFREY: Another important feature of the Japanese market is how both consumers and opinion leaders in the market tend to accept "conventional wisdom" or *joshiki* - also translated as "common sense" - but in my usage it's the generally accepted explanation for why things are how they are. I don't mean that there aren't an equal number of independent thinkers and authentic opinion leaders in Japan as there are in any society. But in general, you find that some phenomena, such as consumer spending patterns, are explained by so-called experts. They then get repeated and the vast majority of Japanese will latch onto such explanations. Before you know it, it's accepted by all, purveyors and consumers alike, as the accepted truth or conventional wisdom.

There are many examples of how new technologies or new business models are initially rejected out of hand in Japan for no other reason than what I call the "JID principle", the belief that even if it has worked somewhere else, "Japan is different." I encountered this directly when I began pitching the IMAX cinema multiplex model to Japanese cinema chains. Even with a proven business model for stand-alone IMAX mega-screens within Japanese museums, aquariums and Expo sites, the idea of retrofitting multiplex cinemas was a big "we don't believe it will work here" and "multiplexes are different in Japan." This was at a time when IMAX had already taken off in most other markets around the world.

Eventually change happens. In the case of IMAX, it took a leap of faith by 109 Cinemas (Tokyu Recreation) to open the first multiplex-retrofitted IMAX in Kawasaki. We were very fortunate with the timing and run of movies the year we launched in 2009: first *Transformers* in the summer, followed by a one-month run of Michael Jackson's *This Is It*, and the original *Avatar* after that. *Avatar* in 3D, in particular, was hugely popular in IMAX and we had a very long run, followed by another major 3D success: Tim Burton's *Alice In Wonderland.* IMAX itself is not really about 3D, but the whole experience of seeing it in this amazing new large format with unusually powerful sound just blew people away. By the time *Avatar* had released we had opened four IMAX locations in Japan, and with that film alone we earned $8 million on those four screens. That's $2 million per screen! All of a sudden, IMAX experienced a huge paradigm shift and everyone wanted to be in the IMAX business.

This pattern - of initial resistance, or conventional wisdom to explain why "Japan is different" and will not work in the market, then followed by eventual adoption - is very common.

Smartphones are another great example. Initially Japan was ahead of the rest of the world with a self-contained mobile internet environment in the late 1990s from DoCoMo called i-mode. The rest of the world had something called WAP (wireless application protocol) for early generation mobile phones. i-mode combined a wider array of internet standards including email, web access, and packet switching data delivery to give users access to all sorts of information and services. It was a huge success and future competitive iterations of it brought what came to be known as "feature phones" – often flip phones with larger color screens with everything tailored to Japanese consumer needs. These phones were really quite advanced compared to what was available elsewhere in the world. Then SoftBank bought and rebranded Vodafone and within two years obtained the exclusive rights to the sell Apple iPhones in Japan. Consumers were initially slow to start buying them, using the commonly accepted explanation that feature phones cover all Japanese needs and "smartphones" were never going to break through. Initially many would buy a smart phone and keep the feature phone for their uniquely Japanese benefits, carrying two phones, but the thinking started to shift as more and more apps were introduced that enabled smartphones to do an even better job than the feature phones. Once that happened, the market changed rapidly. It's the same story with many things.

You can see a similar phenomenon in the music and home entertainment businesses where CD and DVD rental shops have persisted for so much longer than anywhere else in the world. Not just rentals, but sales of CDs and DVDs. Here it likely has more to do with the fact that CD and DVD sales in Japan always went above and beyond other markets in terms of the quality of packaging and presentation, and bonus features such as unique Japan-only CD bonus tracks. The Japanese almost always get quality and presentation right and often teach the rest of the world how to do things for the future - just think of the high quality of vinyl records that, in their day, were sought after by enthusiasts around the world. But another factor for CD and DVD rentals was that rental shops were located near train stations, and consumption patterns meant that people were used to stopping by their local rental shop to choose something to fit their whim on a given day. The *joshiki* or "conventional wisdom" was the same: Japanese consumers prefer buying and renting the physical formats because it fits their preferred experience of the entertainment.

The history of pay-TV in Japan is another example of how entrenched local players - in this case national broadcasters and advertising agencies - stubbornly protected their most profitable revenue stream: advertising. They created their own ratings agency called Video Research and adopted a "Gross Rating Points" (GRP, or household ratings) system. This contrasted with the highly segmentable and sophisticated "Target Ratings Point" (TRP) system already being used internationally and allowed the agencies and broadcasters to extract higher profits. Buyers could still follow somewhat loosely tracked TRP ratings and try to buy based on those, but it was a guessing game, and the actual pricing was still based only on the GRPs.

Then in the early 1990s when pay-TV was introduced in Japan, the powers-that-be used Video Research - a *de facto* monopoly - to thwart foreign upstart ratings agencies. It was the same old "JID mentality" that Japanese major advertising buyers preferred to buy based on GRPs. The agencies and national broadcasters limited the share of advertising revenue going to the new pay-TV channels by restricting their access to ratings data. When they launched their own satellite channels they relied more on subscriber revenue than advertising to protect their lucrative terrestrial channel bread and butter. To this day, whereas cable and pay-TV thrives in the US and represents a large share of TV ad spends, in Japan FTA advertising for the five commercial net- works still represents 85% of all yen spent compared to 15% for all the pay-TV platforms combined. It took the arrival of non-ad- supported streaming services like Hulu, Netflix and Amazon to shift the paradigm. These heavy-hitting newcomers are exploiting the decline in quality scripted content from Japanese broadcasters and investing big time in ambitious local content projects. Add to this the growing popularity (and ad revenues) of user-generated content (UGC) platforms like YouTube and you can see major change is coming.

So, ultimately, while the powers-that-be thought they had won the battle with pay-TV, actually they just created a weaker, hollowed-out broadcasting industry.

As with IMAX, smartphones and traditional home entertainment formats, eventually Japanese consumers begin to see the attractiveness of services other than the incumbent players. As noted above, a big game-changer was premium content streaming services which fell outside the broadcast licensing system. I remember being dumbfounded that we could set up Hulu Japan in 2010 for a launch in 2011 as a nationwide service for the television viewing public without any licenses whatsoever!

When Netflix launched in 2015, the conventional industry thinking was that it was destined to fail. They said Netflix may have effectively started local content well, but they don't understand the Japanese market. What they vastly underestimated was the power of scale as a worldwide company with over 230 million subscribers in 190 markets and a rapidly growing library of strong and varied original content.

To be fair, even Netflix originally didn't realize how valuable this would be. About six months after I finished my work developing and launching the Hulu Japan service (still the only international launch for Hulu) I had lunch with Ted Sarandos, then the Chief Content Officer and currently the co-CEO of Netflix. I wanted to see if Netflix might be interested in developing Japan. That was in late 2012 and at that time he told me that Netflix had no plan or intention of ever entering the Japanese market, saying it was too difficult. It would be another two years before Netflix decided that an all-or-nothing worldwide strategy was required, and they did hire me for a time as a consultant to advise them on content strategy.

Netflix initially may not have had as strong local content as the local competitors such as Docomo's dTV or U-NEXT had, or even some services run by the Japanese FTA broadcasters, but it was just a matter of time and their level of effort. All Netflix needed was to get the premium content version of what is known in the tech world as a "killer app", or a show such as *Terrace House* to make a name for itself. In the case of *Terrace House* they were able to establish it as a top show not only in Japan but also in markets like the US. Showing that Japanese content could become popular in other markets proved to local producers that Netflix had what no other local player could offer. In the five years prior to 2021, Netflix had gone from being the 5th or 6th-ranked service with only a 4% or 5% market share, to being number one with 20%. They literally swapped positions with DoCoMo's dTV service, which now is in 5th or 6th place with only 4% or 5% market share but five years prior was number one with 20% market share. A true reversal of fortune! It shows the importance of committing to a long-term plan, unlike Hulu who were not prepared to do so.

I believe, ultimately, good business models and good services will succeed in Japan, but there is usually initial resistance. Japan will often lag behind the rest of the world except in cases where it is the originator of a technology or business model. On-demand streaming, for example, Japan was about seven years behind the rest of the world.

Whenever I pitch a client wanting to enter the Japanese market - irrespective of how great their business model might be overseas - I insist that they buy into the three principles I outlined above. That is, that they commit to a long-term plan, they have a Japan-specific strategy, and they be prepared to question wisdom. I often think that if Hulu, who were first to market, had followed these principles like Netflix did later, they could be the market leader now, provided they also pursued a bigger worldwide strategy. When I look at another recent client such as Warner Bros. Discovery's Max, I believe they can still succeed as others have done with the right worldwide, consistent, and dedicated long-term approach.

4
- Stephen Cox -

"The crux of it was getting people together in a non-threatening environment, with tact and with the intention of having fun."

Profile

Stephen Cox has lived and worked in Japan for over 30 years. Most of his career has been in the communications and media industries and his expertise is leading and guiding international teams to achieve relevance and success across cultures and languages. He joined BMG Music in 2000 as Senior Director, New Technology, Asia-Pacific to spearhead the development of the company's global music digital and tech strategy and its implementation in Asia-Pacific. In 2004, he joined a leading 90-person Japanese digital agency as a Board Member and Executive Officer to lead the business planning and implementation function to transform and grow the company. He served as Chief Strategy Officer, Executive Officer at MRM (McCann WorldGroup) from 2007, before joining the Vivendi Group's full-service global advertising company, Havas, as CEO/Representative Director and President, Japan where he worked for eight years. He was responsible for tripling revenue and profit and doubling the size of the operation in Japan.

Frank's Foreword

I had worked with Stephen Cox at France-based Vivendi Group. He was the Japan Country Manager for their marketing and advertising company, Havas, and I was at Universal Music Japan's merchandising company, Bravado. I was always very impressed by Stephen's keen insights on the cultural aspects of doing business in Japan. He is also one of the most eloquent speakers I know, so I was very keen to talk with him for this book.

Interview

FRANK: As a marketing and advertising agency, your relationships with your clients are obviously very important. Can you start by talking about any challenges and solutions in that area?

STEPHEN: When I joined Havas Japan, from a global perspective, our customer relationships were poorly managed. Neither our account managers nor our client brand managers were operating to globally accepted (or more accurately "western") best practices for planning and executing marketing and advertising campaigns. Best practices, which were defined and agreed contractually at a global level for how we would work together, were not being implemented in Japan. The big cultural reason behind this was actually of our own making, and not uncommon among western brands operating in Japan. Brands tend to bring in a highly experienced head office person who is very well ensconced in their industries and in their brands and in their products coming in from overseas, but they rarely have much deep experience with the Japanese market, or consumers. Among other challenges, this usually leads to hiring practices that don't take into account a fundamental difference in the talent development here. Japanese companies tend to hire at a much more junior (entry) level and then build up the skill and career of employees over decades and across many divisions internally. So, the western company thinks they are hiring a trained brand marketing specialist or brand design specialist from a big Japanese brand like *Kao* or *Lion* but what they are getting is a generalist who had gone from division to division, and who might have been in marketing for just the last two or three years. They'd learned a little bit about marketing Japanese-style there, and they had enough on their resume to be brought in as an assistant brand manager or even a brand manager. Mistaken expectations about what the talent market looked like and the kinds of people they would be able to hire reasonably, create their first problem.

FRANK: More specifically, what sorts of problems does that create?

STEPHEN: There are industry standards for developing advertising campaigns that are basically accepted by global companies. You start with a concept, based on research and market understanding, and you gradually refine that concept over time using different tools and processes. It was clear to me from how my team were going back and forth with the client, and from the demands coming back from the client, that neither side was behaving like professional marketers. They simply didn't know what the process was for designing an advertising campaign or a marketing campaign. They had never had an MBA-type template program to follow; they had never been trained on a formal robust process at *Lion* or *Kao* or wherever they were coming from on how to make a TV commercial or an advertising campaign. This is largely because in Japanese companies the job of developing marketing tends to be the work of the advertising agency. This is very different from western agencies which tend to demand a lot more from their clients: "What do you want to do? What are your objectives? How do you want to express it? What does your brand mean? What is your brand strategy?" In Japan, these are questions that the company would give to their agency, and the agency would figure it out and come back with a recommendation.

So, the expectations about the relationship between the brand and its advertising agency differed between the western-trained client management and the local client *genba* level staff. And in terms of the hiring (and talent development) there were different expectations as well, so there were people coming to us and making demands that weren't in line with management's perceived professional standards.

FRANK: How did you go about fixing this problem?

STEPHEN: The first thing I did was to convince my global management to give me a liaison officer. I hired this young guy from Havas in Hong Kong, who was very wired into the global group. And together over a couple of months we built a full-on, three-day workshop on TVC (television commercial) development best practices for the client's marketing team. We offered this as a free service to the client, and I had our own brand managers attend too, so they were learning these skills at the same time. So just five or six months after I joined, we ran the first big workshop for the client. We made it fun and focused on a few core points, and kept it simple, which really helped overcome the cultural barriers of understanding. We relied a lot on reverse role-play where we put our creative director in the role of the client and the brand manager in the role of creative director or strategy director whose job it was to come up with the idea. It was very interactive and included brainstorming on solutions, which normally does not work in Japan, but because we included so much fun stuff and we weren't highly critical, it turned out to be a very successful program.

Within a year, Japan went from second to bottom of the client's markets to the top ten in terms of great evaluations. During this shared experience between us and the client and between our local people and their non-local people, we were able to overcome a lot of skill-based and cultural-based challenges that had previously impeded the adoption of global best practices in Japan. From then on, the relationship just got better and better and more profitable without having to win more business from the client.

FRANK: So, if you didn't know Japan, you wouldn't even have understood the problem, never mind come up with an appropriate solution.

STEPHEN: Yes, you're right. The assumption by top management was that we've got brand managers in place in Japan, so they must know what they're doing. In fact, in the Japanese environment they did know what they were doing. They were probably effective brand managers in the setting of a large Japanese brand, but not in a global agency-client environment.

The core difference is that – particularly in North America, but also in Europe in a slightly different way – there are very robust templated ways of designing, building, and implementing communication plans and marketing strategies. In the west, people learn all of this in MBA programs and the like before they join a company as a marketer. They will also go through on-the-job training to learn the specific templates and procedures for their company. And there's an assumption that because that works so well across so many markets it will work the same way as well in Japan, and it doesn't.

One of the big cultural differences is that major Japanese brands pride themselves on the fact that they have internally built their processes and approaches for whatever function, whether it's advertising or human resources or product development. It's all internal. It's their own experts that have built everything up, and their own experts are generally lifetime employees, so they haven't experienced how it's done in other companies. When a western company comes into the market and is looking for these experts, they are hiring from a talent pool that is structured and trained differently. If you don't have someone with some authority in your organization who understands that, you will get into serious trouble in Japan!

The other related issue is that the Japanese staff who were trying to express these challenges and problems to the global and regional teams had only ever worked in the Japanese market and weren't able to articulate the issue in a way head office could understand. They were very smart and usually linguistically articulate, but it's almost like asking a fish to describe water or trying to describe air to a fish.

FRANK: As Country Manager, what sorts of skills do you need to deal with this situation?

STEPHEN: Whether they are Japanese or western, you need somebody who has a foot in both worlds. I guest lecture in various university MBA programs and talk about "absolute" and "relative" facts. For example, "The United States has 3.5 million square miles of land" is an absolute fact, and "The United States is a frontier-based economy" is a relative fact. It's true in relation to Japan, but it's not perhaps true in relation to Australia. But you can only make those comparisons and understand the difference between relative and absolute facts and perceptions when you have a foot in both worlds. And for me, when you are talking about management across cultures, you must have some segment of the organization that has a foot in both worlds. Otherwise, you cannot understand those differences between the facts that people are presenting, the relative facts which you only understand when you see both sides of the equation, and the perceptions, which you can only understand if you've got all that behind you.

A lot of the problems that I had with global colleagues and clients were related to their preconceptions about Japan. One was that technology-led communications and strategies would work in Japan. They had very high expectations for programmatic marketing from very early on, before anybody in the Japanese market really knew what that even was. Those perceptions led to a lot of trying to put square pegs into round holes. Globally we had this magnificent programmatic advertising tool, which we were using in many markets. I remember one person even saying, "We're using it in Singapore, and that's the same as Japan. We're using it in India, so why shouldn't it work in Japan?"

But the advertising agencies and the publishers that you had to connect with to run programmatic had never heard of it, so you can't do it. That's a perception-based issue because people don't even relatively understand the position of the Japanese market.

So, if you present these as facts to somebody who has been in the Japanese market for their entire career, it doesn't make any sense, there is no context.

IBM and Microsoft were renowned for developing and rolling out what were called "global programs." But in reality, they were just US programs rolled out globally. They just didn't make sense. I had a similar challenge with my company's mostly French brands, that we had these powerful, robust programs that worked very well in markets throughout the world but were *non sequiturs* and almost meaningless in Japan.

Faced with this cognitive dissonance, the approach I took was to educate the clients' global teams. They were very receptive because Japan was a big - usually the second biggest - market in the world for some of these brands. For example, in the case of a major international airline, the global CEO and the global heads of communications, advertising and marketing, and their teams were active participants. I designed a half-day workshop for them, where I talked about some of the causes of reasons why consumers see things differently and have different expectations from an airline, and why JAL and ANA market the way they do. When these global people looked at the advertising and marketing of JAL and ANA, they couldn't figure out what was happening. "Where is this brand coming from?" "What does this brand mean?" "What does it offer?" "I don't get it." After doing this first set of workshops for global management in Japan, they asked me to do that on a regular basis three times a year for different people within their organization. So, three times a year they would send out the Head of Airport Lounge Experience, the Head of In-Cabin Experience, the Head of Reservations...

all these different functions, to go through Stephen's half-day workshop on developing all the aspects of the product for the Japanese market. My only regret was that I didn't charge them for it!

That allowed us to do two things with the client. Firstly, it allowed us to tailor the global communications to be relevant for the Japanese market, and secondly it enabled us to do something that was forbidden globally, and that was to develop independent "for-the-market" communications on a local budget, which their local people in Japan had always wanted to do. The net result was that we were able to grow our business with them.

The crux of it was getting people together in a non-threatening environment, with tact and with the intention of having fun. We were painting the pictures of the cultural differences, not specifically between Japan and another specific country, but between cultures more broadly. This could only be done by somebody who had a foot in both markets.

FRANK: People often talk about the very different communication styles between western cultures and Japan. What is your experience in that regard?

STEPHEN: A very common situation in a western company in Japan is where it looks like communication is happening but it's not. And it's usually because the Japan side does not push back: they'll accept, even though they know it's not right, even though they know it's going to cause all sorts of problems that they'll have to fix. And because they are not pushing back, the other side thinks, "Ah, they're agreeing." The western side is not hearing the non-verbal communication that is screaming at them.

You will often hear people talk about how for Japanese, "Yes" means "I've heard you," it does not mean I'm agreeing with you. But what is far less discussed is the western tendency to project in these situations. Even experienced Japan-Insiders, including myself, are guilty of this. One thing I noticed constantly happening with people coming in is that they would quickly talk about the challenges or the solutions, and in an almost cursory manner say "Do you get it? Do you understand?" to which the Japanese person would make a positive gesture. That was enough for the (western) side to assume that everything that had just been said, and all the underpinning context behind it, was understood. So the incoming person, speaking very quickly, assumes that they've got their entire message across, even if only 10% of the message was actually articulated, and only 50% of what was articulated was understood. It's a two-way thing.

FRANK: So how did you address that?

STEPHEN: I found that workshops work very well because you state something, and then you have it stated back to you, and then you go through it again. So that, by the end of the process, both sides have re-stated and re-confirmed and re-formed, and come to an agreement about what it is they are talking about. The challenge is that Japanese people are not as accustomed to doing workshops as western people are. So, you have to make it very non-threatening, very friendly, with lots of breakouts where it's two people talking to each other before they have to speak to the whole group. And it also means that when you are working with western people, you have to be sure that they are not just projecting or shooting out their viewpoint or their information or their agreement or their disagreement... they are checking and confirming it to make sure of what was said, and what was heard. And that's on a person-to-person basis in a workshop, and it's on a brand-to-consumer basis in communications as well.

And I think this is true irrespective of industry or business type. Ultimately, business is just "person" writ large, especially when you are talking about the part of the business which is communicating to people in order to move forward - ensuring stakeholder agreement, understanding and the insight so things move forward strategically.

FRANK: To make an impact, you must ensure that the change doesn't just happen when you're in the room, and I think that's what you've done. By changing the culture, you've actually created sustained change.

STEPHEN: That's a great point. In my budget meetings at Havas we typically had several guests from global management and regional management, including the global head of HR or the global head of a client segment. We all loved to talk about profit and about growth, but what I was trying to build was sustainable value for sustainable growth. Havas – well, all corporations - are very good at jumping up and down excitedly and getting into mutual admiration parties, about one-off firework type achievements, which are important when you go for the low-hanging fruit in order to motivate your team and your wider organization. You need to have those quick, high-profile wins, but if you only focus on that, your business is going to zig-zag from minor success to minor success, not building a foundation for sustainability.

So you have raised a really important point which is not always addressed. That is when western companies - who have all these robust structures behind them - come into the Japanese market which doesn't have the same robust structures in place, everything has to be re-aligned to somehow sync. Sustainable growth is about looking for the cause of "why" things are, rather than trying to fiddle with the effects, or change the effects by fiddling with other effects, which is like a doctor treating only for symptoms and not looking at the cause of the disease. So, the symptoms disappear and you're feeling a bit better, but a problem arises in another part of the body because the cause has not been addressed, and the actual disease is getting worse.

FRANK: This must have been very confusing for your staff.

STEPHEN: Yes, it was. In fact, many of the local staff didn't understand their roles and priorities. They were aware of the problem, but they didn't know how to fix it - what they should be prioritizing, what they should be working on, what they should be providing. This was because many of them came from other foreign companies and understood what was expected of them working in a western company, but our company was being managed in a very Japanese way. And I'm sure you've seen it in HR or any team, a Japanese boss will give a "do this!" or "make this!" sort of instruction, but will generally not tell their staff how to do it, or exactly what the output should look like, or how they will be judged on it. It's basically "do this and figure it out!"

I remember joining NYK (a shipping company) as a new recruit nearly 30 years ago. And it was training by osmosis. I was put in the HR division, then the PR division, and then I was put in the operations division, but every time I would be given a task with no instruction how to carry it out - no instruction on who to talk to, where to go for the information on past cases - you were expected to figure it out. And that is, or was, pretty common in Japanese companies that form the standard of Japanese business management. So managers are not good at mentoring – or maybe they mentor but they don't train, task, or evaluate very well by western standards.

When I entered Havas at the beginning, there were people who were doing everything they could, but 80% of it was not aligned to the objectives they should have had, so things were becoming unprofitable, the quality was bad, and people were not being evaluated. They didn't know if they were doing well or not, they didn't know how to develop or move up the ladder. The reason I was hired was that the staff had basically revolted. They told the regional manager that they would all quit if they didn't change the CEO, which pushed regional management to look for someone.

FRANK: That's pretty serious! How did you avert the revolution?

STEPHEN: When I come into a new situation, I try to manage expectations. I take anywhere from two to six months just to get my feet under the table and understand the situation. I found two big staff-related issues. One issue was widespread lack of trust - in the company, between staff and management, and among staff themselves. The other issue was inappropriate allocation of skills to tasks. For example, account managers were doing copywriting, copywriters and designers were managing client expectations. There was no system, and there was no evaluation process, so nobody knew what they were supposed to be doing. This was odd because Havas globally was actually very strong in this respect.

So, the first thing I did was build a robust evaluation system. I talked to every employee, every manager, to find out what their hopes were and what their clients' expectations were. I'd do a preliminary evaluation and I'd say, "Over the next three months, try to achieve this, and over the next six months try to achieve this, and we'll look at how far you've succeeded on those at the end of the year to determine what your assignment should be, and what your salary should be." It was complicated by the fact that, due to bad business results, the previous leadership had cut everybody's salary and then promised to reinstate it - when a certain point was reached - but this never happened. But it meant that after six months I was able to have a reassessment. I adjusted the goals because some of them were just not as achievable as they seemed six months earlier when they were set. This reassessment gave clarity of expectation and clarity of path forward to staff who did not have the benefit of either robust western HR practices, or the vaguer but implicitly understood Japanese practices.

The next step in getting people to stay with the company was to enthuse them about going through the Havas training programs: Account Management 101, Design 101, Strategic Planning 101. All these training programs existed globally, but they needed to be tailored to the Japanese environment. Localizing the training programs took a long time, and it was a continuous process. You could never take your eye off the ball. Because if you did – and it happened to me a few times at Havas – things would get bogged down in a rigid western template style of managing staff. Or they'd spin off out of control. I ensured that new people coming into the company understood that this was the way things worked, and these were the expectations.

The theme through everything is constant communication, at every level. Relentlessly coming back to every point that you've communicated, and talking about how you can evolve - "Have we succeeded? Do we need to continue with this? Or is it finished and we can move on?" - on every single point.

Once we had addressed the big client problem and the internal staff problem, suddenly our core stakeholders could see light at the end of the tunnel and be happy. Both the clients and our own staff were enthusiastic and talking. We won new work, we were working smarter, and, as a result, quality was improving. It took one full year, but for the first time the company achieved a robust profit. Once that was done, then came my big challenge: talking to my boss and head office.

FRANK: OK, so what were the issues there?

STEPHEN: When I first joined Havas, I was faced with big challenges and high expectations, but I had absolutely no autonomy. Every single thing I wanted to do I had to run by my regional boss. I couldn't hire, fire, give raises or promote people. I also couldn't change the way we defined our services, which was a key challenge - we weren't defining our services correctly either for the global service package or for the local needs. My boss, who was a very good boss, said, "Stephen, the first thing you need to do is achieve profit. If you have profit in your back pocket, you have credibility to get autonomy to do it the way you think you need to do it."

Gaining autonomy, in terms of redefining the scope of work we were doing for global clients outside the global contract, was critical for me. There was a disparity between the global and the local offering. That was also the case for our clients in terms of their own product offering in Japan. Early on at Havas, there was a very narrowly defined set of services that we were to offer as an advertising agency. So, for one client it was all about TV commercials, and in the years before I was there, they would build 30-second TV commercials for the market even though the standard was 15 seconds. It's difficult and very expensive to buy 30-second spots, and consumers don't react well to 30-second spots. And they are a lot more expensive to create. But for several years, Global could not imagine that a 15-second TV commercial could work, so they didn't allow it.

On a wider level, we needed to be offering services around experiential, real events in the streets, combined with digital advertising. Pop-up events are very big in Japan for introducing products. We needed to be able to offer that sort of thing, because you are in a city where over 3.5 million people pass through a single train station every day, so if you have an event in Shinjuku Station, you're already reaching a huge audience. With such a dense audience compressed into a small space in Tokyo, you just need to do a couple of pop-up events and you have the equivalent impact of three million dollars of TV time.

That's because there is no other city in the world where some seven million people travel into and out of the city every day through a small number of bottlenecks. That makes them very easily reachable, with impact in short time, for comparatively little cost through experiential and digital promotion, which is very different to other markets. That was one of the reasons why I started Havas Digital, Havas Health, and Havas Content as subsidiary companies. They represented opportunities which were being offered in Japan differently or to a higher degree than in other Asian markets.

If you can understand how consumers access information during their day - checking out on their phones where they are going to have lunch from their office - that's an engagement point with a lot of reach to consumers for a whole range of products from luxury to FMCG.

It sounds obvious, but you can't market effectively if you don't understand the market, and the market is defined by the people who live in it. People who live in the Japanese market, being relatively homogeneous, have some very clear specificities. If you address these specificities correctly, you can achieve a great deal. But these specificities are very different from the west.

Toyota spent a lot of money on car commercials that would put the car in a beautiful scene, not actually talking about the car. They would talk about camping. Hitachi would do the same thing. They had their "Inspire the Next" brand-level stories, told in 15-second TV commercials. They wouldn't address product attributes very much at all in the commercial; they'd do that in another area; they'd do that through pop-ups, or dealer fairs, or digital; and there they would be very granular about the product attributes, much more than a western marketing platform would be. Consumers respond to that inspiration and what it represents, and they identify with the brand message, even if they don't explicitly articulate it. It's a different way of approaching the audience because you have a clear understanding of how these consumers behave. Understanding the Japanese consumer in this way is critical to success in this market.

With one UK-based household appliance, we had the challenge that their vacuum cleaner was almost as tall as I am, so it was not going to fit into a Japanese home. And it was really noisy.

I was having these discussions for a long time, and I said you will not have much control over the retail environment, because it will be in large consumer electronics stores where you will have a tiny space with all your home-market competitors ranged around you. Ultimately, they gained the understanding of the market and the retail environment – through UK executives who had gained deep experience in Japan before their appointment. And they were then able to revolutionize the retail environment and re-design their products for the market – achieving overwhelming success in the end. The key points are knowing retail environments, and knowing consumer needs and motivations. Then understanding these in a Japanese context, and finally having a foot in both worlds so you can explain them outwards and inwards.

When we achieved profitability at the end of that first year, I suddenly had the autonomy I needed to redefine our products and services, redefine the scopes of our global clients, and redefine the local work we were doing for global clients outside the global contract. By defining what services we provide, we could determine the expertise we need in-house and what our profit levels were. Costs were also down because we were taking less time to do everything, and this enabled me to renegotiate global contracts as they related to Japan. Because - again - global contracts were often made with little understanding of the local situation.

The trust that was gained by managing these local specific problems of internal trust, and the way of managing resources, and the way of managing clients, enabled me to gain the trust I needed to do things the way they needed to be done in Japan. And that was the key to unlocking the business.

One of the reasons I left Havas was because that boss left. There is a saying: "You don't leave a company, you leave a boss." I was lucky that I had a very good, open-minded boss. He was Chairman of Asia-Pacific based in his native Barcelona. But he was emotionally very much invested in Asia-Pacific. He loved the region including Japan and would visit three or four times a year. He spent a lot of time here. He spent a lot of time with the team and would remember everybody's name. And he had a very good understanding of the Japanese market, as well as China and other Asian markets. He was a terrific ally in explaining where markets were coming from, with a very strong understanding of the Paris head office's cultural expectations. This was very important because Havas, global though it may be, is a very French company.

5
- Jeff Daggett -

"You have to make them feel great about their successes because monetarily it won't change their life. The monetary benefits will accrue to the company."

Profile

Jeff Daggett has over 30 years of experience in building successful, profitable brand and content businesses in Japan and the Asia Pacific region. He pioneered the Japan retail launch for Gap, Levi's, Nike and other brands, and grew business now worth over $1B in annual revenue for their owners. He has grown consumer products businesses for Disney, NBC Universal and others in Japan and Asia Pacific, and generated over $300 million in royalty revenue for brands and content creators. Jeff is the founder of Aisonne, a brand and retail development and management company that has assisted Apple, Columbia Sportswear, Nordstrom, Shinjuku Takano, NBC Universal and others since 2002.

Frank's Foreword

Jeff and I come from similar work backgrounds in brand and character licensing. We both headed licensing operations for popular kids' and apparel brands. But his businesses were considerably bigger than mine, so I was interested in comparing notes to see how the big guys did it!

Interview

FRANK: How important do you think cultural sensitivity is for foreign companies coming to Japan?

JEFF: Cultural sensitivity is important, but you must put it in context. There's a tendency for international companies coming into Japan to take the mission of cultural sensitivity so seriously that they arrive almost wearing kimonos. I had done some work in hiring Japanese sales teams for Apple Computer working in Japan's big box electronics retailers, before Apple had their own retail. This led to an opportunity to do an orientation session for the incoming Apple Store team in Cupertino. They had just come out of cultural sensitivity training, and they were wrapping their minds around changing the things that they'd been told they needed to change to succeed in Japan.

My view is a little different in a couple of ways. The first point is that you never mess with your brand values. There is an authenticity to entities, just as there is an authenticity to individuals; and you don't want to mess with that to fit in. The second point is that if you are successful in somcthing in your home market, don't change things before you meet "Japan". Meet the market, have the conversation firstly with the teams that you hire, and then, if there are things that need to be changed, like accommodating a longer sales cycle, etc., then do that as needed.

The example I use with my American counterparts is how Japanese companies adapted when they went to the US. There is a Harvard Business School case study known as "Honda A vs Honda B."[48] There are two stories of how Honda came to dominate in the US. The Honda A story fits the traditional "Japan dominance" narrative of the 1980s: they pre-planned everything and they knew exactly what they were doing, and they came and kicked Harley-Davidson's butt. The Honda B story presents a different scenario, which is that when they came to the US with the Super Cub, they quickly learned it couldn't handle the longer distances and was breaking down. They had to airfreight them back to Japan overnight for analysis and re-design to survive the conditions in southern California.

There is probably some truth to both stories, but I think the more compelling one is the iterative process in Honda B. Apple actually had the same experience in the US. It's not a revolution but an evolution. So, come to Japan and evolve, but don't have a revolution because someone in the team said you need to completely upend your business to succeed in Japan!

When I started with Disney, the US and global teams were adamant that the brand could only succeed in the children's category. That we have a 2~5-year-old customer and beyond that, there is not a lot we can do. The very clear message was, "don't put your energy anywhere else; we want to strengthen the infant and children's business we have; just focus on that." But we were learning otherwise in Japan, through our experience with Disneyland which had been in Japan for almost 25 years. In Japan, the parents who had taken their children to Tokyo Disneyland in 1983 were now grandparents, and the kids that they took were now adults with kids of their own, but they still loved Disney product. What we discovered, and it was an evolving process, was that Disney could work with adult product.

But we were strongly discouraged by the US from doing that. The US was not wrong; that was their lived experience in the US at the time. But, of course, they have since evolved too and the brand has a much broader customer base.

The great thing about this is that you can bracket markets by where they are in their development stage. For example, in India character merchandise is still considered to be very much for children. The market has developed in its own way, but it hasn't moved along the continuum of a more adult consumer-experienced market like Japan, though that is starting to change.

Looking at the market in Japan, you may find opportunities and niches that may not exist in the home market but are worth trying. Because it's a licensing business, we were able to experiment in a low-risk manner to slowly grow older demographics. During my time with Disney Japan, we grew the adult business from less than 10% to 60% of revenue. This is actually an example of a few times when Japan became a global leader for new trends in the business.

FRANK: Do you have other examples of when Japan led global trends?

JEFF: When I was at Nike, the company was very serious about establishing and maintaining its athletic credentials. That was in its DNA, but it was also seen as having grown up in the shadow of Adidas which, as the makers of the original football shoe, were seen as owning the serious athletics segment. Nike was known as a serious player in running footwear, which was the lion's share of their business. In Japan, we knew there was an opportunity in casual footwear, but it was really difficult to pitch this is to the Nike footwear gods at head office! How we dealt with this was by, over a period of about three or four years, nurturing a redefinition of what "an athlete" was.

This was no easy feat. You've got to understand that the head office shoe team were all athletes themselves. I didn't realize how significant that was at the time because I didn't have that athletic background, but for these people, first and foremost, answering an athlete's needs was the priority. The attitude was "if you're not on the field with a professional sports team, you're not an athlete; or you could be an athlete but we're not going to put you in any commercials." Head office had world-champion runners on staff.

Where they began to let the light in was being willing to create shoes that an athlete, or even a non-athlete, would find comfortable just walking around town in. You might not be wearing these shoes to shoot hoops or do cross training. You might not be running in them, but just wearing them as casual shoes.

So, over time, we got the marketing team around to the definition of "athlete" being: "if you have a body, you're an athlete." Initially there was some resistance to that, and a great deal of resistance around marketing because there was concern that doing something that looks more like fashion would damage Nike's athletic credentials. But to Nike's credit they tried it. It worked, and it didn't dent their athletic credentials in the areas where they were strong like running and basketball.

That allowed for a lot of things that turned out to be great opportunities in Japan, like a more casual shoe. We launched a product called the Nike Presto. It was a global launch and did especially well in Japan. It became something different in Japan because there was a strong fashion sense and a fashion community. Also, it was released at a time when the AirMax 95 had already established Nike as a fashion footwear brand. It was so successful in Japan that Uniqlo eventually copied it!

FRANK: What was the dynamic like within your team throughout this process?

JEFF: The situations at Nike and Disney were both driven by a healthy sense of urgency across the entire team; not one that is abusive or where there is power dynamic in play. There was some stress involved, but above all we were motivated by a positive sense of urgency. It wasn't existential per se but there was a feeling of sink or swim. We didn't know how far we'd have to swim, but we knew we had to do this right now. Everyone involved knew that it would make a big impact on the business if they succeeded. This is an element of the evolution and, where necessary, the reinvention that must exist in successful teams. The Honda B example had that.

FRANK: Listening to you talk, there are so many parallels with my experience with Thomas and Friends in Japan. You've reminded me of the initial resistance to things like making Thomas cuter to expand the demographic to infants. It meant changing the creative look by removing hard key lines, making the eyes less piercing, and generally softening the look. It took time to convince them but, just like your Disney example, the Japanese designs crept into other markets too.

JEFF: Yes, we often made the eyes bigger to appeal to the cute-loving audience in Japan.

FRANK: There were also differences in thinking about taboo categories. I remember being summoned in front of the CEO at one point because we approved Thomas toilet paper. It was actually a very popular licensing category for kids' brands in Japan because parents used it for toilet training. For the guys in the UK, it seemed like we were soiling the brand!

JEFF: I had the same experience at Disney and at Universal. Toilet paper and feminine hygiene were a big "No." Despite the category serving what is considered a normal bodily function in Japan, it didn't matter how many "Hello Kitty" feminine hygiene pads I would show people, the reaction was almost puritanical: "We can't approve this, it's unclean!"

FRANK: What I guess we're talking about is the importance of understanding your customer (who may be different from customers in other markets).

JEFF: This was often the challenge I had with some of my colleagues, not just in Japan but also when I was working Asia Pacific, I had to try hard to explain the scale of some of the opportunities in the region. And to be fair to them, I had my blind-spots too and I had to be convinced of things, and there were things I didn't get. But one of the struggles that I had was market understanding – for example, the potential and importance of the Indonesian market. The way we language things - the words we use - directly impact the concepts we are willing to entertain and the possibilities we allow to be created. Just by naming a region like Asia as "Australia and other Asia" in your presentation materials, the sub-text is that we don't know a lot about Asia, and you've eliminated the possibility of addressing a market where potentially a lot of future growth will come from.

FRANK: How have you gone about building trust with your teams in Japan?

JEFF: If there was one principle that people going into business school or coming out of business school should be aware of, it is this: as a leader you are always responsible. I see a lot of businesses right now saying it's perfectly fine to have 101 excuses for why it's not our responsibility. It's important to remember that you can delegate authority, so that if something goes wrong it might be because of something someone on your team did, but it's still your team. So, responsibility starts with me and ends with me. If we can do that, then we build trust with our team.

You put a little bit in the favor bank; you give credit, and then when stuff is not going right, you as the leader take the heat. You are seen by the team to be taking the heat. You can have the side conversations, like the failed engineer when the space shuttle blew up: "Nobody's bad here, but our space shuttle blew up; there are some things that now have to happen. Unfortunately, this is the situation. I am responsible but this is a challenge for all of us."

You need to have these conversations, but being responsible sets you up to do that. And to never be the person who leaves the team out to dry.

Let me give you an example from NBC Universal where we spent quite a sum getting one of their kids' brands on TV Tokyo. Some of us had experience with this model from Disney days so had reasons to believe it would work. The mistake we made was underestimating the fragmentation over time in the attention span of kids. Nickelodeon had realized this, and they were putting their content on YouTube in shorter segments and, obviously, viewable at any time. The only way our content could be seen was on our very expensive appointment viewing on TV Tokyo. It wasn't a disaster, but it didn't do what everyone thought. Yes, everyone was onboard with the plan, but I was the boss, so I took responsibility for the outcome.

FRANK: We actually did the same thing for Thomas and Bob the Builder. We took on the risk for a 30-minute slot, and then, with Sony Creative, we sold the advertising and got support from TakaraTomy and some of the other licensees. Our ultimate goal for Thomas was to get on NHK, so we needed to keep the show on terrestrial television somewhere after we were dropped by Fuji TV. Everyone understood the goal, so the licensees stayed on board.

I'd like to ask you about "risk-aversion" in the context of managing people in Japan. Somebody put it to me that the issue was not so much "risk", but "uncertainty." What do you think of this distinction?

JEFF: I agree, and more specifically, "How the uncertainty will unravel and affect my career." In a lifetime employment situation, there is not a lot of room for error. Even the smallest mistake can have serious repercussions for a career that is already limited by your annual 3% increase, your interdepartmental transfers, or being sent to Dubai for three years with no real clarity on the corporate development journey.

Incentives and risks are not aligned in the Japanese employment model. There is a lot of risk for not a lot of incentive. The only way you can bring people along is to give them psychic returns. You have to make them feel great about their successes because monetarily it won't change their life. The benefits will accrue to the company. But if they screw up it will slow their advancement and will negatively change their life.

The Japanese employment model is slow, steady promotions, no superstars called out or paid that way. You're a tortoise and not a hare. And that's how the HR department will develop your career. It's how your compensation is going to increase. In order to make sure everyone is treated fairly and equitably, if everyone is treated as a tortoise, then nobody is ever caught out on anything.

FRANK: So, is HR the problem?

JEFF: No, I don't want to single out HR. They are managing to a broader social contract, which is how Japanese staff want their careers managed. They don't want to find themselves suddenly unemployed, so they are willing to go with the slow and the steady because it means in a bad year their employer is going to stick with them.

The other thing I would highlight in terms of engaging your team in change is to really focus on communication. We think our job as a communicator ends when we hit the "send" button, but that's really where it starts. A wise leader once taught me, and I will be forever in his debt, that when we communicate it's not what we say, but what people hear. You have to make sure that your team understands what you are saying, to the extent that they are repeating it back to you. That does not mean that they agree. You have to create a safe space where you say, "We're not looking for agreement right now, we're just talking about what our alternatives are. But here's what I think is important for the brand, and why. Do you understand that?" And then, "What do you think?"

Paradoxically, the fact that everyone's on the tortoise path in Japan is what creates all the opportunities we have to do amazing things. The excitement that comes from a career is not going to come from getting a bonus big enough to buy a house in Hawaii. It's going to come from small wins in the office. Most people do not want uncertainty because they have had no positive experience from it. And so, if you can create a positive experience around small changes, you can build trust to implement larger changes. A cynic is simply an engaged optimist whose heart has been broken!

Once you've built real communication and trust around small victories, you can start to ask if there is anything else we are willing to challenge. Through ongoing communication, you're telling your team that, yes, we have a lot of uncertainty, but risk is inherent to our business. You are constantly managing a lot of risks - merchandise risks, real estate risks, financial risks, systemic risks. Risk is intrinsic to our business. And what you're trying to convey is how to manage these risks intelligently. We'll get it wrong sometimes, but with good planning we'll get it right more often. You open up a dialog with them about, "what risks do we as a team want to sign up for now?" And if we are not ready to sign up for something, and if the business allows you, as the boss, to look into that later, you start with things around which you can get a consensus. If you're listening, I think people are pretty good at telling you what their appetite is and how much uncertainty they are willing to take on.

6
- Giles Duke -

"It's often said that Japan is weak in the face of gaiatsu. *If used judiciously, it can be very effective in achieving the desired outcome."*

Profile

Giles Duke has lived and worked in Japan for 50 years, including nearly 30 years in the music industry. He has worked both in the studio - with artists as diverse as the Yellow Magic Orchestra, Sheena Ringo, and the Kodomo Band - and on the business side - including stints in business development, marketing, and HR. His career includes terms with major labels such as BMG, Sony, EMI, and most recently Universal Music LLC where he is currently working as a consultant. In 2021 and 2022, due to his extensive HR experience in supporting people, he was the Executive Director and Advisor of TELL - the lifeline, clinic and outreach NPO serving Japan's international community.

Frank's Foreword

I wanted to talk to Giles about achieving change at a Japanese company for at least three reasons. The first reason was because of his deep understanding of Japan and Japanese culture, having lived and worked here for most of his life. The second was his decades of experience in the Japanese music industry, estimated to be worth $7 billion and the world's second largest music market. And the third reason was because of his interesting blend of experience across both business development and HR, which gives him a unique perspective both on high-level business strategy and on everyday staff behavior.

Interview

FRANK: How different is Japan in the global music industry?

GILES: Traditionally, the Japanese music industry has operated in a very different way from the west. Powerful artist management companies and talent agencies have been able to call the shots for years. This means that the process of signing artists, for example, typically takes much longer and requires more compromises. There is greater disparity between royalties for physical and digital products, where the physical royalty could be 8% but the digital royalty could be as high as 40%. Management companies will insist on a significant advertising spend before they will sign on the dotted line. The way master rights are handled is different. In Japan, the label will typically give the master rights to the band for the first two years before being transferred back. These are just bridges you must cross; there is really no negotiation about it. If you don't accept these terms, they'll go down the road to Sony.

FRANK: From a cultural perspective, what challenges does this mean for a non-Japanese Country Manager?

GILES: The cultural skill is knowing when to push for change and knowing when to accept the Japanese way. This is why at EMI we brought the whole process in-house. The talent managers were our employees, and the artists were our artists. Having your own label artists in your own management company is one way that record companies are trying to break the hold of the *jimusho* - the powerful agencies that manage most artists. Sony did the same, and the stranglehold of the agencies on talent is diminishing. You see the same in the TV world where the talent agencies have been weakened because terrestrial television networks nowadays are not as strong as they used to be.

FRANK: Has this impacted consumer behavior?

GILES: As with other countries, technology is forcing fundamental change in viewing behavior. A lot of young people don't have TVs in their rooms and are very selective in what they watch. It's usually driven by something that's happening online, and increasingly by Netflix and other large-scale streaming companies. There are still some strong agencies, like *Amuse* for example, but they are very proactive and constantly looking for new opportunities before other people see them.

So, yes, while some old habits die hard in Japan, when you look at how young Japanese kids use technology to access entertainment, there is a significant convergence with western cultures too. They don't know about analog TV or a world where there were only five terrestrial channels. They only know a digital world where content can be accessed in many ways. It's actually a good time for the music industry because there was a moment in the music world where Napster disrupted everything and let people download illegally. But now it's provided through legitimate platforms like fee-based streaming services or ad-based platforms such as YouTube for free - if you don't mind being interrupted by all those commercials! So, this generation now has access to all this content legally through their phone, through their devices, in the same way that that's driving everything in Los Angeles, in Sydney or in London.

But even with these fundamental changes in consumer behavior, internal resistance to change is quite common in the music industry. There is a notion that "it has always been done this way." We had a situation in Japan with a senior finance person refusing to comply with certain company-wide processes, insisting that "that's not how it's done in the Japanese music industry."

FRANK: So, how do you deal with senior staff who are resisting change?

GILES: One thing I have found that works is *gaiatsu* (pressure from outside). It's often said that Japan is weak in the face of *gaiatsu.* If used judiciously, it can be very effective in achieving the desired outcome. I remember at one company we had an issue with a senior finance guy in Tokyo. He simply refused to comply with certain global reporting requirements. We tried everything we could locally but eventually we decided to engage the regional CFO in Hong Kong. He tried to deal with it by email first, but eventually ended up coming to Tokyo to deal with the situation face-to-face. It probably sounds a little extreme, but it's what we had to do to get him to cooperate.

I had another case where our global CEO was a marketing-oriented guy and he wanted to use data-driven marketing. And he was right! If you're selling the Southern All Stars you need to specifically target the audience who buy their records. We employed a terrific person from a global consumer brand who was a specialist in this type of marketing, but she got a lot of resistance from the traditional sales and marketing guys who were all about ads in magazines and billboards in front of Tower Records. Eventually it took intervention by the CEO from overseas to crack down on the old guard and allow her to get things rolling.

FRANK: Is there any other advice you would give foreign companies and Country Managers with respect to making change?

GILES: In many organizations in Japan, resistance to change is often coming from individual senior managers. They are used to controlling their own departments and are reluctant to move towards a more collaborative and transparent work style. Something that I have found to be very effective is to adopt a data-driven and transparent decision-making process. The overseas CEO I just mentioned was way ahead of the game. He is famous for renewing a contract with Pink Floyd based on his data-driven approach. They were bowled over. They said they had never been presented with material like this before, and it was what they'd wanted for the last 30 or 40 years.

I had a somewhat similar experience when I was working for EMI Japan and we merged with Universal Music Group. EMI was at the forefront of the move to digital. A lot of our processes were already digitized, and we could see that digital distribution of music was the future of the industry. Universal, on the other hand, was on the way there, but hadn't yet reached that point. It was difficult to capture sales data, for example. You had to apply for it and only later would you get it. At EMI we had our own system, where you just accessed sales data through a portal using the product number. It was so obvious which was the more effective system and within two months of the merger the Universal folks decided to use our one, and the merged company now uses a more-improved version of it. I think the best system will always prevail in the end, because you just can't argue with results.

If there is a silver lining to Covid in Japan, it's that it forced companies to digitize their products and their processes. And because they don't have a lot of expertise in this area, they have had to work with foreign companies which exposes them to even more new ideas which I think is a very good thing!

7
- Harold Godsoe -

"In the American context, the lawyers will call the sheriff's department to take action. But in Japan lawyers don't have any recourse to apply power or force. There's no sheriff's office, no way to push someone to do what they don't want to do. Because basically people always do what they are supposed to do."

Profile

Harold Godsoe is a U.S.-licensed Canadian business lawyer specialized in servicing international subsidiaries in Tokyo. He has lived and worked in Japan for 12 of the past 20 years, with half of that time within a unique mid-sized Japanese corporate firm. His advice is underpinned by having previously lived in several different countries, work within NPOs, and as a legal advocate advising for and against major governments in areas including international trade policy and special economic zone design. His experience in providing legal services in Japan ranges across manufacturing, services, food and beverages, and cutting-edge technology law.

Frank's Foreword

I had listened to Harold's interview on Clubhouse before I talked to him, and enjoyed his clear reasoning and deep insights. He stressed the importance of approaching people in Japan as honest actors, and with an assumption of trust. Through personal experience, and from other observations from my business career, I had come to believe that trust operates in a different way in Japan from overseas. Given Harold's background in philosophy and law and his work in several countries and various legal systems, I wanted to know his views.

Interview

FRANK: In your Clubhouse interview, you began by talking about trust. You said that the premise for business in Japan is to approach people as honest actors and not as rival players in the game of business. Trust, you said, is something that exists between people, and a legal contract is just a tool that expresses that trust. Trust, of course, is a universal concept but it's also very subjective. What underlies trust in a Japanese context?

HAROLD: In general, a lot of trust is based on how you handle yourself when you are powerful, and I am not. I learned at some point about hunter-gatherer societies that have a ritual called "insult the meat." They use it to deal with the spike in hubris that a skilled hunter gets. Before a feast in which a butchered animal is eaten, the tribe insults the meat in front of the hunter who killed it. "What a pathetic animal. It must have been so slow. It's almost all bones." Everybody recognizes that they are having the feast because of this hunter's skills, but the hunter is not allowed to let his spike of success go to his head, or he won't be trusted. I think there is a similar dynamic at work in Japan.

Japan is known as a collectivist society and there is a reason for that. There's a sense that if you try and stand out and, especially, abuse your power or skill in even subtle ways, the people you are inflicting your power on will just hint behind your back that you're outside the circle of trust. And pretty quickly there is a whole group of people who think you're a bad actor, the air thickens around you, and you're not only not trusted, but you're also not powerful anymore.

I've seen cases in Japan where people - usually Americans - arrive with a power and insistence. "I'm right. The law is on my side. I have the money. I want this contract fulfilled, or my rival in jail." But what happens is that the authorities, or whoever, will decide that you are a troublemaker, outside the circle of trust, and they will only do the minimum to help. Because, in Japan, the troublemaker is the problem.

The same thing happens in company-to-company dynamics. With very few exceptions, if your average American or British large company takes the position that, because they have a little more power or a little more clout in their home market, they can force Japanese partners to bend to their will, they will simply be stonewalled. They can't understand why their power is not being respected because, in western culture, water always flows downhill. In American culture, if a company comes in with the law on their side and the money on their side, everyone just buttons up and does what they are supposed to do, even if it doesn't feel right. But that doesn't happen in Japan. The water doesn't flow in the same way. You're swimming against the tide; it doesn't matter how strong a swimmer you are, the Japanese tide will take you where it wants.

Counterexamples are also interesting. Sometimes Japanese try to raise that tide against power, and nothing happens. It causes a kind of stalemate if no one makes the next move to show that they are the trustworthy party. I was working on a local subsidiary company that was being liquidated, and the members of the subsidiary were just stubbornly refusing to let it happen. The overseas head office had all the power (and a legitimate reason). But the local Japanese staff weren't leaving the office, they weren't handing over keys, they weren't doing any of the things they are supposed to do by law and by company policy. So, we engaged lawyers in their town, locally, to handle the situation; to talk to the employees individually. We found that the local director was the one abusing his power, painting the head office unfairly as abusive and arrogant, and it helped the rest of the employees to see that the head office was going to have local support. The tide wasn't going to go in the direction they thought it might. The local director was isolated, and the problem solved.

The same thing happens with the eviction of commercial (and residential) tenants. There is nowhere (for a landlord) to go to force a tenant out; people can squat. They can stop paying rent and squat for months or years. The best way to approach the problem, which still leaves me a bit cold, is to get inside their lives – speak reservedly and reasonably about the situation to their bank, and their customers, and their family. Squatters take on their own kind of position of power, so you need to obtain the trust of the people around them, and then raise a tide.

To give a different kind of example, I know of a case where a Japanese company was courting an overseas company as a distributor in a new market. They spent about a year negotiating back and forth. The foreign company was strongly advised to give the Japanese company time, that it takes them forever to make a decision, but that when they make decisions they act quickly. The foreign side heeded that advice and everybody was cordial and positive. And then "Bang...!!" The Japanese company bought a rival company, poured all its energy into this acquired company, and just started tearing apart the market. This completely broadsided its erstwhile partner. The foreign company thought the Japanese were aimless and indecisive. My guess, in that case, is that the Japanese company was taking the normal amount of time to decide whether - after all the profit calculations - the foreign company could be brought inside their circle of trust. But the Japanese company also earned a reputation from that situation of being quite vicious and cut-throat. Not at all the normal stereotype.

FRANK: I've experienced that myself when I was running the Thomas the Tank Engine business. I thought we had a solid relationship with our broadcast partner and was confident that we were well inside that circle. But unbeknown to us, they wanted to allocate our afternoon slot on their network to a potentially higher-rating domestic show. They identified a loophole in the contract that allowed them to shift us from their top-rating free-to-air channel to an obscure satellite broadcast channel. That really took the wind out of me. It was like I was acting like a Japanese person, and they like a foreigner. I just didn't think business was done like that in Japan.

HAROLD: Sometimes foreigners exploit this. It's called "playing the *gaijin* card", when they are requested to do something and they just say, "No!" And the Japanese side doesn't know what to do, because you're not supposed to say no in that situation. There are supposed to be consequences if you don't do what you're trusted to do. Nothing bad seems to happen initially. Maybe *gaijin* don't know what they should be trusted to do? But something bad does happen eventually. The reputation of somebody who says no at the wrong times is damaged, and it will cost them in the future.

There are always exceptions, but in general, in the American context, the lawyers will call the sheriff's department to take action. But in Japan lawyers don't have any recourse to apply power or force. There's no sheriff's office, no way to push someone to do what they don't want to do. Because basically people always do what they are supposed to do.

FRANK: I had a situation when I was working in publishing where the big Japanese publishers were seemingly unable to do anything about a high-profile counterfeit Japanese *manga* website reportedly run by organized crime. Our solution was to take action outside Japan. We had our head office in New York tell Google that unless they (Google) delisted the Japanese website and made it unsearchable, that we would take action in the US. This killed the pirate's ad revenue and the site disappeared overnight.

HAROLD: That's close to my experience, too. When you need to spend social capital and bring big guns, sometimes it's best to go to the American head office.

FRANK: I'd like to ask you about the role of empathy in Japan. But first a little background. I have been involved in two traffic accidents in Japan over the years. In the first, I was legally deemed to be in the wrong; and in the second, the other person was deemed to be in the wrong. What surprised me in both cases was that the police encouraged both parties to talk directly. This seemed counter-intuitive to me. I figured I'd be putting myself at even more risk if I openly admitted guilt! In the accident where I was in the wrong, the policeman gave me the injured party's number. It was late at night so I said I'd call in the morning. But he said no, call now, the earlier the better! I did as he advised, and it worked. Despite suffering a painful fractured rib, the man thanked me for my concern and actually told me he wouldn't be taking any legal action. It happened again the second time around, in reverse. In retrospect, I now interpret the police officer's advice as being motivated by empathy. A feeling that you'll get a better result if you try to imagine how the other person sees it. Would you agree with that?

HAROLD: I think that's a beautiful side effect of the way collective society works. I've seen that many times; it's definitely a common experience. But I've also seen many counterexamples where empathy is withheld. Empathy is something that's traded as part of a strategy to achieve harmony. But there are situations where collective harmony can be achieved without there being any empathy at all. For example, the border situation during Covid. There is not a lot of empathy for anyone who is negatively affected by that. The government has managed to achieve total harmony, even if it has had to cut off its nose to spite its face. If you shrink the circle you achieve collective harmony, but there's nothing for people outside the circle. But in that car accident, the policeman made sure that everyone was inside the circle. If you shrink the circle, you achieve collective harmony, but there's nothing for people outside the circle.

FRANK: Being inside or outside the circle - is that what it comes down to?

HAROLD: Yes, especially, for example, a Country Manager who is coming in fresh. It's so easy to isolate an expat Country Manager from the company, especially if they have been sent for a limited time like one or two or three years. It takes a lot of immersive work to get inside the circle, and, even then, the door can be slammed shut by one bad move.

FRANK: I had a brush with a "one bad move" situation when I was running Japan operations for a major kids' brand. We were working very closely with an excellent Japanese master licensee. They had represented the brand for years and had established it as a top three kids' brand, which is no mean feat for a foreign brand. They were one of the best partners I've ever worked with, real honest actors.

Then at one point my company's private equity owners in London decided to take tighter control of the global business. They replaced the CEO and COO in London with their own appointees and started to make changes. One of the things they wanted to do in Japan was an audit. This was not a bad move in itself, but it was the way they approached it. They started from a position of distrust and treated people with suspicion from the outset. I remember one meeting when the interpreter caused a stir when he used the word "kickback" in English for *kikku-bakku* in Japanese. I interjected to clarify that the Japanese word meant "commission", not an illegal payment as it does in English. Such was the level of distrust from the PE-appointed lawyer that he accused me and our master licensee of corruption. Talk about a bad move! Fortunately, my relationship with our Japanese partner was strong enough to keep me within their circle, and I still work with them today.

If you're a Country Manager and your default position is to trust the people that you work with, would that help put you inside the circle from their perspective?

HAROLD: Yes and no. That default assumption may work if it's guaranteed that you are inside the circle. If you are not inside the circle, it (the assumption) goes. I've seen trusting Country Managers completely cut off from everything that's going on in the company. Employees can be dishonest with the manager, for example by just going along with things until they have an opportunity to complain to the head office. There's no loyalty in these situations.

When I'm advising somebody to proceed in good faith - for example, when two companies come together in a joint venture or a distribution agreement - my assumption is that you are already in the circle and you won't step outside. When you are in a joint exercise, you are probably in a good situation and can safely assume that everyone is acting in good faith. But if you are on the edge of the circle, your priority should be to get inside it. And don't assume good faith until you are inside it.

At the root of every society, everybody has at the back of their mind the final consequence. In the American context it's usually the sheriff, which is a gun. You will be removed, forcefully if necessary. Somebody is going to show up with a gun to enforce what is collectively desired.

In Japan that force element has been shrunk to basically just anti-social and criminal elements, who don't appear to do it very well! The consequences in Japan are exclusion from the circle, leading to things like overwhelming depressive shame, which is pretty bad. Everybody wants to be liked by everybody else at the end of the day, so, if you don't want to be homeless and shunned, you follow the rules. Between the two, I rather prefer Japan. I wouldn't say it's a better system, but it's a more positive environment to live in.

8
- Ruth Jarman -

"There was so much miscommunication that the US side actually started thinking that the Japanese side were lying to them."

Profile

Ruth Jarman first experienced the energy and grit of the Japanese business environment over a 4-year stint with Recruit Co. Ltd. starting in 1988. In 1992, she launched her first business in Japan translating and interpreting for high-profile clients such as the Rev. Jesse Jackson, Monica Seles, and Joe Montana. She later joined Space Design KK where she worked on a daily basis under the mentorship of the legendary entrepreneur and founder of Recruit, Hiromasa Ezoe. In 2012, she established Jarman International KK and currently works with a host of major Japanese clients such as MS and AD, Shimada Group (owner of Hotel and Residence Roppongi), JR East Kikaku, Cosmo Oil, Tokyu Construction, Kochi Prefecture, and Yonezawa City. In recent years she has also been focusing on helping Japanese companies wishing to expand into the United States. Ruth also serves as the first woman/international Outside Director for two Tokyo Prime Stock Exchange listed companies, KADOKAWA and Fujibo Holdings. Ruth also holds the Takken Japanese real estate license (this Japanese certification only has a 13% pass rate nationally).

Frank's Foreword

I had been a big fan of Ruth Jarman having heard her speak many times on a range of topics related to doing business in Japan. I was especially interested in talking to her about three of those topics. The first was her experience with communication challenges between foreign and Japanese partners. The second was the cultural aspects of project management in Japan. And the third topic was about managing and mentoring her all-female team at Jarman International KK.

Interview

FRANK: What do you think are the biggest challenges for foreign companies doing business with Japan?

RUTH: The biggest challenge for foreign companies in Japan is communication. Let me give you one example. An American company was bidding for a United States' military contract and they wanted to include some Japanese technology in their submission. They need to figure out how to partner with the Japanese company, how to go after the bid, how to divide responsibilities, etc. There were lots of meetings, or virtual meetings since Covid. But there was so much miscommunication that the US side actually started thinking that the Japanese side were lying to them. That's when I was called in.

The first thing I realized is that very little was being recorded in minutes or even emails. It was all verbal. What emails did exist were just exchanging pleasantries like "the meeting went so well," so everything looked positive and constructive. So the US side would say, "OK, good, go back and ask them for their quotation." In one email, the Japan-based representative of the US company wrote, "Dear Mr. Tanaka, As agreed, can you get us the estimate by tomorrow so we can clear this with our head office and take it forward." Tanaka-san's response, of course, was, "No, we never said that!"

This happens all the time between Japanese and non-Japanese companies. The Japanese side is saying things like "*hai!*" and "yes" and nodding, and the non-Japanese people interpret this as agreement. I had to explain to the US people that this didn't mean their Japanese counterparts were onboard with what was being said. They were just acknowledging that they understood what was being said. And then I had to explain to the Japanese side how their comments were being interpreted by the Americans.

The key thing was to coach the Japanese side on how to respond in a way that didn't cause misunderstandings. So instead of "*hai!*" and "yes" and nodding, I advised them to say something like "this seems like a good idea, but we need to discuss it internally before we can make a decision." This enabled them to make it clear to the other side that they understood what was being proposed, and also to flag that it was something that needed further consideration. I also advised the American side to get somebody on their team who can speak Japanese, because there are so many cues, verbal and non-verbal, that are very different between cultures.

Clarifying, always clarifying, is critical. But you need to do it in a way that doesn't make the other side feel that you are ridiculing them. One thing that Japanese companies do very well internally is to minute meetings (*gijiroku*). They circulate the minutes and everybody must sign-off on them. A lot of times the reaction in the US is "why do we need minutes? It's, like, so yesterday! We recorded the meeting; why would we need minutes?"

I think having a written record is very important. They can be in English or Japanese, it doesn't matter. The other side can always get it translated. Within a reasonable time after the meeting, have everybody sign-off on what was said. They do it at the board level, I'm sure in the US too, so why not for important negotiations like these. I think it's well worth the investment.

FRANK: I know what you mean. I once worked on a brand and content licensing project with Lady Gaga's management office in LA. By the time I joined they were at the approval stage which was incredibly detailed. But, just like your example, most of it was done on conference calls and the detail wasn't being recorded. The first thing I did was create a database that captured all the project elements and tracked the approval status.

RUTH: I've noticed that since Covid Japanese companies are much more comfortable with online shared documents than they used to be. There's always a danger with Excel sheets going back and forth that you lose track of the most recent version. Shared documents make it so much easier to track who changed what and when. So, also using a shared document for the minutes makes sense.

Project management is very different in Japan. As with anywhere, the KPI is to finish on time but there is a tendency here to drag out important decisions until the last minute and then scramble to finish. It'll be all-hands-on-deck and overnighters and the like. This is especially true with what I call "soft projects" like, for example, an idea-related project. In manufacturing you can't do that because you have predefined processes and specifications to follow. But on a soft project where there is so much emphasis on consensus it can take forever to get started.

Everyone knows that there's a hard deadline in two months, but they just keep on talking around the issues, and the project keeps getting pushed back or de-prioritized.

So, my solution was to treat soft projects as if they are a manufacturing job. I define the project specifications clearly in a shared document with day-by-day calendar. I have clear red lines showing milestones and deadlines that must be met. I tell my staff to avoid taking phone calls from the client to avoid the potential of important information not being recorded. It really is so easy for mistakes to be made if you rely on verbal communication. We train our clients to communicate by email, unless, of course, it's a true emergency.

Conventional wisdom in Japan is that you should respond within 24 hours. I don't agree with that. Obviously, you read emails as soon as they come in, and if you are towards the end of a project and a really important email arrives, well... yes, responding within 12 hours or even one hour is really important. But I tell my staff that, as a rule, respond within 48 hours, and never respond right away. Unless you do this, the client will assume that you are on call for them, and then if you don't respond within three hours, they will start wondering about you and worrying if you are seeing their mail or not. That then leads to a call. I use a lot of strategy in how we communicate and manage expectations with clients!

FRANK: What is the cultural element to all of that?

RUTH: There are two things at work here. One is that in Japan you are supposed to respond within an hour to everything, to any mail or phone call. The word in Japanese is *sokutaiou* (immediate response) and it is greatly valued by the customer. So the default mode of most Japanese staff is to respond quickly. The other factor here is that, because consensus is so highly valued, everybody must have some input. This might have an advantage if it's a tangible item where you can see the shape and the mold and the process. But if you're talking about an idea, it's unmanageable. In Japan you tend to get too many cooks stirring the broth. And then somebody says, "By the way, the deadline is next Wednesday." Then there is a flurry of panic to get it done. My company can't and won't work that way. I put a lot of effort into coaching and changing the habits of my staff in this regard. It's very important, especially since most of my staff are working moms.

FRANK: Could you talk more about how you manage your local employees?

RUTH: Most of my staff are women. In general, these ladies join via introduction from someone already working with me and have pretty much no previous leadership experience at all. They are used to being asked to do tasks and to sit in the passenger's seat, rather than accepting responsibility to get things done. The reason for this is that, as women working for a Japanese company, they have never been considered as potential leaders. They are trained to do tasks, and they do them really well. But what happens is that completing the task becomes their goal. What I need to teach them is that the real goal is to close the deal and get the money coming in. Not just do tasks. You have to flip their priorities to being more goal-oriented. This is a huge hurdle in trying to grow a company in Japan.

My first step is to "filter out" people who have no interest in assuming responsibility. And it's really hard because I can actually see their potential - maybe as a terrific project manager, or a great *kacho* (section manager), or even as my successor - but they don't see it themselves. What I'm looking for is people who are not afraid of making mistakes. That's rare because Japanese women have always been told that they can't make mistakes, that making mistakes is the worst thing. I find that 80% of the Japanese women I work with are much happier and much more comfortable just doing tasks.

In my experience it takes about two years to figure out whether a person is management, project management or leadership material. As I said earlier, every single one of them has the potential. The challenge is getting them to believe it themselves. I don't want to use the words "step up" because doing tasks well is a recognized and valuable function. But sometimes, as their boss, I feel so frustrated because I see their potential. Many of them could be the main breadwinner for their family if they wanted to be. But getting them out of where they believe society has put them can be very hard and takes time.

And when I do finally find the right person, I ease them into their new role slowly and gently. I start raising their pay significantly, and, over time they start to realize that they have the potential to make even more money and have more independence. It's not all about money, of course. They also then start to get respect from the client. And they start to see that if they close this deal or lead this project, they have the potential to advance even more. They start to notice women in other companies operating at a high level and follow them as role models. It's a slow process, but, without question, well worth the effort.

Every Japanese woman has the capability to lead and manage. They already have the core skills. They are leading at home, they are raising their kids, they are managing the household budget, so the ability is there. But in a business situation at your typical Japanese company, they won't be given the opportunity. I would like to think what I do is empower them to realize their potential. I want nothing more than for the ladies I work with to step up and say, "I want to do this; I want to make some money."

All my staff work from home. This does present some challenges such as building team spirit and a sense of identifying with the company. But it has benefits too. They have more control over their work/life balance, which is important because most of them have children. It also cuts down on the in-house drama that can occur when women start bucking the system and taking on leadership roles on projects and over other staff. Of course, we have to interact often on projects, but there is no pressure to be "best friends" as well as colleagues.

There are all these unseen societal pressures and restrictions on women in Japan. The men don't have a curfew, they don't have to go home by the last train; in fact, they are encouraged to be out late drinking. There's pressure on men too, but nothing like the level experienced by women in terms of what they need to get done every day and the chores at home. I've often advised women to set up their own separate bank account for their salary. It's not always the case, but I have seen cases where it caused issues at home when the wife started to out-earn the husband. When women are told "you could do it if you worked harder," it's a totally legitimate choice for them to say, "I'd rather just focus on the tasks."

FRANK: I'm interested in your comment that your staff don't identify strongly with your company. Can you talk a little more about that?

RUTH: I believe that Japanese working women in general do not identify with their companies. Their identity is with family and kids. This might change in 20 years or so, but for now that's the case. If they have kids, it's about how they are doing at school, if they are being a good mother, if they are doing the right thing - a good mother not in the sense of, "Do I love my kid enough?" but "Is my kid going to get in the right school or university?" If she doesn't have kids, she still doesn't identify with the company. If she's single, she might identify with her parents, or her outside activities, because in Japan it's still not the norm for a woman to identify with her company. If a woman said, "I love my job so much. My job is my life and I don't do anything else," people would say, "What about a husband?" Or, "Don't you want children?" The view is that that's not a legitimate life-choice for a woman. Maybe I'm expressing it too strongly, but it's what I believe is the current reality here. I am doing my part to try and challenge this status quo.

From childhood, women in Japan learn that their role is to be useful to others. When you say *tasukarimashita* (that was a great help) to a Japanese lady, she's much happier than if you say *arigatou gozaimasu* (thank you). That's an important point to remember and it's such a societal difference. Being appreciated in that way is the goal that has been implanted in Japanese women's minds. That's how they know they have been useful. I hope this changes because I don't think it is good for the business environment. For me as a western woman, I feel it very *wagam-*

ama (self-aggrandizing, arrogant) to say that. But it seems to be something that Japanese women really respond to.

FRANK: Japanese labor law makes it very tough to dismiss staff. How do you deal with non-performing or disruptive staff?

RUTH: You need to make it their decision to leave. The deal at my company is that the longer you are in the company the more responsibility you get. So, if you want to get rid of somebody, you have to wait until the next fiscal year starts, and you say, "Now you are in your third year, and you are going to have these additional responsibilities and manage these people, and these are your new tasks because you are now a *senpai* in the company." Somebody who is lazy and doesn't want to do that will quit. That's the way you get people to quit; you just give them more work, based on the societal rule of more responsibility as your seniority increases.

FRANK: What is your advice to consultants or potential Country Managers when talking to foreign companies looking to enter the Japanese market?

RUTH: The many experiences I've had with managers overseas is that they literally do not believe what I'm saying. They don't believe. It's not trust. It's as if I said, "I've just turned this water into wine. Will you believe me without tasting it?" The reason is because "Japan" is so not in their experience in most cases.

So, laying down conditions is very important. If a foreign company is asking me to help them launch in Japan I will tell them things like they must be willing to invest $250,000 every year for the first five years even if there is no result; they must set up an office (even a shared office) in a central Tokyo location; they must be prepared to send a senior-level person here at least every three months for two weeks each time for clients and the like. So, what I'm doing is testing their commitment and weeding out the companies that are not really serious about succeeding in Japan.

I am very careful about introducing foreign companies to my Japanese network. If things don't go well, it's my reputation on the line. It's a slightly different context, but one technique I've used to mitigate risks when introducing a foreigner that I think could help with the project is to first bring them in for a seminar in front of my Japanese client. I'd suggest they do a speech on a certain topic or have them come in for a meeting. I notice that if you bring them in gradually, step-by-step like that, it is a good risk hedge for people like us who are trying to grow companies.

In one example, I was working with a huge insurance company running professional development seminars. I also had other projects going and needed to get some help in. What I did was use one of our seminars to ease in the help I needed. I had the client select speakers from my network of 50 people I knew would be good to talk about the topic at hand. They chose three people. Sign-up went very well. We had about 300 people online. The speakers were really good; they prepared well, and it was a huge success. A little later when it came time to bring in the additional people, the client stipulated that they liked two of the speakers, who they mentioned by name, but they didn't mention the third person. They were saying "we want somebody not like that other person but like these two people." So, through this audition-like process I was able to onboard people I knew would work for the client and mitigate any reputational risk for myself.

9

- Alan Malcolm -

"Head Office had no thought for the damage they were inflicting on our Japanese partner and on the brand in Japan."

Profile

Alan Malcolm has been working with people and projects throughout Japan and the greater Asia region for over 20 years. He specializes in sales, marketing, online media, negotiation, HR, professional development and general management. His industry experience includes over ten years at the helm at Pearson Educational Publishing in Japan and APAC, where he led the growth of online automated communication skills assessment products in partnership with the Nikkei Group. This led to an opportunity with Nikkei as Chief Commercial Officer of their corporate training company, Excedo. Alan is now Japan Country Manager at ACE, a boutique administrative services firm specializing in assisting businesses with their international expansion.

Frank's Foreword

I met Alan in 2017 through an introduction by a mutual colleague and friend. I was immediately impressed by his rich experience with joint ventures between major international and Japanese educational publishers and, more recently, in cross-cultural professional development and Japan business expansion. I was interested in hearing his stories of challenges, solutions and successes, both in terms of the company-to-company dynamics and local team management.

Interview

FRANK: Let me start with the same question I've asked several other contributors. What is it that the foreign Japan-Insider Country Manager can offer that a Japanese national or a head-office secondee cannot?

ALAN: I think it is the ability to know when to challenge the status quo, and when to accept the Japanese way of doing things. In a high-context and old culture like Japan there are a lot of assumptions embedded in everyday thinking. Sometimes they are there for a good reason and must be respected. But sometimes they need to be challenged in the culturally appropriate way. Let me give you an example from publishing. The standard industry discount in Japan was 35% and every company, including the foreign publishers, offered that. There was no question it was high and needed to be challenged. The Japanese publishers' position was "we can't ask for a change, it's always been like that!" On the other extreme, there were publishers from outside the region who sent their regional guy in to hammer on the table and demand the same discount they were getting in the US. Our approach fell in the middle. We negotiated a smaller change but also had them add extra value such as a marketing or promotion commitment.

In my view, if you challenge the assumptions in a sensitive way, and show that you understand the market, people will engage and you will achieve the best result.

FRANK: I had a similar experience with character brand-licensing. In Japan, royalties are calculated on the recommended retail price, rather than wholesale price as happens in just about every other market. The reason for calculating on the wholesale price overseas is that it's easier to audit based on invoiced value. Obviously, you can't control retail prices, so the number is more variable. So, we had people from head office coming in insisting that Japanese licensees change the accepted industry practice just for us. We agreed with them that we needed to be able to do accurate audits, but their proposal was clearly crazy. We worked with our Japanese licensees and came up with a way of verifying the audit based on retail price. There was a solution there, but the immediate approach in head office was to insist that Japan conform with the rest of the world.

ALAN: There is a strong notion in Japan is that prices don't go up. It's almost hard-wired into the national psyche. Head office would tell us for example, that prices are going up 6% globally, so we need to deliver 6% across Asia. With Japan being the largest market, head office wanted to apply as much of the price rise as possible to Japan. On the Japanese side, publishers hadn't even considered that the cost of production had gone up because raw materials costs are increasing! Our distributors were telling us that we couldn't put the prices up because no one else was and customers won't accept it, and they would lose business.

In one recent case I was consulting for a medical devices company. Their sales team would push back on any tiny price raise to distributors or customers even though their company was facing a 40% increase in raw materials and overseas manufacturing costs. Of course, things have changed recently because of Covid and global supply chain issues, but that basic thinking is still there. There is education that needs to happen, and I think us non-Japanese Japan-insiders have a role.

FRANK: So, you can't achieve what head office is insisting on, but at the same time something's got to change, and if costs are going up, some of them must be passed on. Are you saying then that our role as foreign Country Managers is to get that balance right?

ALAN: Yes, and you achieve that balance by building trust. As Japan-insiders or locally hired foreigners, we have a special role in that we are able to build trust in a way that other westerners or expats cannot. Japanese partners look at us not just as someone representing head office, but as someone with a holistic 360-degree perspective. You can see people constructing what I call a credibility index of how much you understand Japan. They'll ask things like, "How do you spend your time? What are your hobbies? What language do you speak at home? Where is your wife from? Do your children go to a local Japanese school?" They're not being rude; they just want to understand you. Of course, no one expects us to be 100% Japanese, but if they see your life is Japan-focused, you do earn some credibility, which leads to the opportunity to create trust.

FRANK: Is Japanese language ability important?

ALAN: Some people think that language ability is overrated, but I don't agree. I strongly believe that for a Country Manager speaking fluent or near fluent Japanese allows you to build trust at a different level with partners and with your own team. There's a completely different dynamic compared to an expat manager coming in. This is probably not unique to Japan, but there is an idea that "if we ride this guy out, in two or three years he'll be gone, and we'll be able to go back to what we've always done." But with the locally hired Japan-insider, they know that we're not going anywhere. We might be here for the rest of our lives!

We are not Japanese, so our initial approach will be different, our culture is different, our communication styles are usually different. But the fact is that we are in the same ship. So, if you can prove that you are in it for the long haul, people will start to open up to you. You will have the opportunity to test assumptions, to talk to people and convince them to give you a chance.

FRANK: You have had some interesting experiences with Japanese trade unions. What can you tell us about that?

ALAN: Indeed, I have had some interesting encounters with Japanese trade unions! In a case at one international company I was running, we had gone through a very successful management buy-out with a Japanese partner. The process was relatively smooth, and we had a good relationship with our management counterparts at the now former partner. But they had a union faction which was not happy. Even after the deal was done, the union was still angry and quite aggressive towards us, resulting in years in the courts. There were occasions when I'd be met by five or six union guys obstructing the ticket wicket at the station where I was trying to get through. They didn't touch me or anything, but they wanted me to know that they were there.

Some of my colleagues had worse treatment, such as threatening messages mentioning where their children go to school. That was scary.

FRANK: How did you resolve that?

ALAN: The same way as you would with anyone: by talking and listening to them. I didn't have problems with the union cause, and I needed them to know that. I understood their motivations, and I talked to them so that they would understand me. This created a space to build trust between us.

FRANK: You've talked about challenges and solutions with Japanese stakeholders. What about head office?

ALAN: Pearson had a strong product which, technologically, was way ahead of its time. It was a fully automated communication skills assessment tool, with voice-recognition and automated scoring delivered by phone or PC. It hadn't taken off in most of the rest of the world but was a massive opportunity in Japan to go head-on with TOEIC. Rakuten was using it and their CEO, Mikitani, was an enthusiastic supporter. The product was scalable, competitively priced, and operationally simple. Even our normally schools-focused publishing salespeople were excited to sell it. With the right amount of localization and the right Japanese partner we knew we had the potential for massive take-up by Japanese consumers. We even had partners who were willing to invest in the development.

But the problem was that head office was trying to launch another somewhat similar product. It was the business version of PTE Academic [49], called PTE Pro. It was a center-based testing solution focused on business English. We knew that we didn't need a high-stakes center-based assessment; we needed a medium-stakes scalable alternative to the TOEIC IP test that people could take on demand. Head office said that our business case didn't stack up. We went back and got more input from customers, we got commitments from a couple of distributors, we tripled the size of the opportunity. But because somebody in the US had done desk research that said this high-stakes solution was a stronger competitor to TOEIC, the Japan team and everything we knew about our customers was deemed to be wrong.

It was so frustrating. We had done our research and even had verbal commitments from corporations that were already spending hundreds of thousands of dollars on English testing. But ultimately it was a case of the head office-based product owner winning the argument over the market owner. It thwarted innovation from Japan. There was a huge personal cost for me too in terms of my reputation and trust with the team. They started to think that if I, as the company president, can't convince the US of something so obvious, then I am not up to the job. I think they felt sorry for me.

Ultimately, people were not comfortable about empowering regions to run their business. I've seen this a lot. Japan is not one of those markets that has been given that sort of leeway. Australia might be allowed to do what they want because they are kind of seen as a safe bet. They've got the right levels of infrastructure, they've got the scale, they've got native English-speaking talent on-board who can articulate very clearly, and they have a sizable enough business for it to tick along on its own. For Japan, it's always "here's a product that's worked globally, now make it work in Japan." The budget for customization is nixed.

FRANK: I had similar cases of opportunities missed over the years. In one case, an editor and I had brokered a deal with one of Japan's biggest publishers on an innovative multimedia science program. The Japanese partner had committed to fund the entire project. Our role was essentially as producer for a share of revenues. The partner was the #1 seller into school and public libraries, which pretty much guaranteed the projected revenues and margins. But it was shot down for reasons that I could only interpret as territorial. The project required collaboration between the US and UK sides of the company and that seemed to ruffle some feathers. As in your case, it had a huge impact on my relationship with the team, and it effectively destroyed a 20-year relationship with the Japanese partner.

ALAN: If there is no process leverage, sometimes you must be a bit guerrilla about it. A last-resort tactic I've used is to invite five or six people from different parts of the company, as high up as your network goes, and get them on a call and spill the beans. It's not a good way to do it and you inevitably burn a bridge or two, but sometimes it's the only way. On the case I mentioned above, I needed the most senior people I could access in Technology, Assessment Product, and English Language Learning, and a regional person who was on the board. I knew from the outset that it would go one of two ways. Either somebody really senior would either tell me to shut up, or would say that "this has legs, let's look into it!"

Your science program in collaboration with a Japanese partner reminded me of a similar case I had. I saw an opportunity to build a cross-cultural communication corporate training program using the Pearson brand and content. Pearson had just acquired a self-study online business English learning company called Global English. It was quite a comprehensive program and market leader at the time. But the brand was unknown in Japan and needed to find a reputable Japanese brand to partner with. I sort of played the *gaijin* card, and made a cold call on Nikkei, the biggest business publisher in Japan, and asked them straight out whether they wanted to create a Japanese version of Global English. Well, it paid off and we created the Global English Nikkei edition. It was a huge success. It went from zero to $2 million revenue in the first six months. It was a high-profile deal and helped me establish relationships at senior levels in the Nikkei group.

The only problem was that I found myself getting closer to the customer than to my own company, which is something I had always warned my team about: "Remember who you work for!" In Japan it's very easy when you're not getting the support from your own side to emotionally align yourself with the customer. Especially when they are saying they are willing to invest a significant amount to drive this business together, because they believe in both the project and you, and can't see why your head office doesn't get it.

Then there was a falling-out between Pearson head office and Global English due to some problem in the acquisition process. Pearson decided to offload the Global English business, without consulting with Nikkei in any way. Initially they couldn't find a buyer and I suggested running it as a Japan entity or partnering with Nikkei. We floated several ideas, but eventually they went ahead with a management buyout (MBO) even though it was a vastly inferior deal than what we could have done with Nikkei which was already a multimillion-dollar customer of Global

English. They basically slapped Nikkei in the face. Nikkei were now in a position where they had to negotiate with totally new owners of a product in which they had invested a huge sum to create the Japanese version. They were the world's largest customer for this product, but they were totally disregarded on the transition and on how things would work post-MBO. They were never even given the opportunity to put their hand up and say they would invest in it to keep it going.

What it came down to was a huge perception gap on the nature of the relationship. Nikkei and I thought it was a partnership; head office saw them as just a big customer. Head office had no thought for the damage they were inflicting on our Japanese partner and on the brand in Japan. If it didn't impact their spreadsheet, it wasn't relevant.

Nikkei probably lost a couple of million dollars in the subsequent years while unwinding their customer agreements. They had sold to some of their biggest customers so there was a knock-on effect to all their other deals with these customers too.

But there was a silver lining to this story. I ended up working at Nikkei again. Despite all the crap that we put them through, they don't blame me or, in fact, my team because they recognized that we were trying to do the right thing ethically. Thanks to the trust built at that time, I've been able to do business with them ever since. They trusted me as a person, they knew that I understood their thinking, their expectations, and their constraints. And the feeling was mutual.

FRANK: You have talked a lot about your team and how you were able to build trust and work well together. But have you had any challenges along the way?

ALAN: Something I've always been vigilant of is that senior management often try to apply a filter when working with foreign bosses. They like to control the flow of communication, both up and down. This is very dangerous. On several occasions, I found I got a very different story from a member of the sales team than I was getting from the sales manager, for example. It seems they feel they have a duty to "translate" and filter the raw data from the *genba* to present me with something I or the regional leadership would like to hear. They assume that we would prefer to hear refined stories rather than the raw truth.

The communication filter is applied at the senior Japanese management level. They are not being vindictive. Their reasoning is simply that head office wouldn't understand if we told them the truth, or that the Japanese team won't respond well to the foreign boss's aggressive expectations. But all it does is create an ambiguous gray zone where goals and expectations aren't clearly articulated, and performance appraisal is out the window because nobody has been told what the expectations of them are. So, you have group targets or team targets or country targets, but the reality is that the Country Manager or the sales manager carries the weight on his or her shoulders on behalf of the rest of the team. In these situations, you do need to put your foot down and insist on a more western-style approach. It's a no-brainer that more transparency in top-to-bottom lines of communication is a good thing.

Another reason this filtering is dangerous is because, not only are you not getting the full picture, but the general staff is probably not receiving your messages either. I work a lot with large Japanese companies and multinationals and it is alarming how many people could not articulate their company's strategy in their own words. I estimate 90% of employees in multinationals couldn't tell you what the strategy was and how it applied to them in their day-to-day tasks.

This is almost the exact opposite of what I was used to at Pearson head office. They had a Chief Strategy Officer who created what he called a "Strategy House" model. It started with the vision and the mission, and how we were going to get there. It came down from the top, so the "roof" was all central Pearson, then flowed down to the pillars which were all product groups and territories. At the foundations there was a space where people could position themselves and the role they played in the organization and indicate which part of the "house" they contributed to. So, they could see, for example, that the role was to create content for a personalized learning experience for a broader number of students in this sector, and it flowed back up. People were very motivated by it. I think they still use it today.

This awareness of strategy, and how it translates into action, needs to be checked on a regular basis. There is always a tendency for sales meetings in Japan to be more about the "story" than the actual numbers. And when you are dealing with head office or regional CFOs who just want to see the numbers, this is a fast track to losing trust big time.

These are things that you only learn over time and through the proverbial "school of hard knocks." In my opinion, the best Country Managers are non-Japanese Japan-insiders like you and I, or if you must have a Japanese person, find someone who's been abroad and has a slightly different experience. Because if you want to understand what's going on with your business in

Japan, you need a Country Manager who is not going to just tell you what they think you want to hear. It happens so often that, say, a regional manager from Singapore or wherever announces to the Japanese sales team that they want to meet the customers. The sales manager's reaction is inevitably, "Why? What is it you want to talk to them about? Do you want to understand if I am taking care of my customer correctly? If the customers do talk to you and they tell you there are issues, are you going to do anything about it?" So, what happens is that the sales manager cherry-picks the customers they'll take the visitor to and controls the information flow that way.

FRANK: I've done that myself! The number of times before my boss's visit we would dress up Maruzen and some flagship stores to look like we owned them!

ALAN: It's a ritual, but it's mainly just a waste of time. The best boss I've ever had was great because he was genuinely interested in what we were doing. He wanted to hear the real story and then he would go away and think about how head office could help beyond what they were already doing. It was meaningful, so I didn't mind taking him anywhere.

10
- Ryan Nelson -

"Successful joint ventures between Japanese and foreign companies are few and far between in Japan, but, if done properly, they may offer a new way to help Japanese companies take some risk."

Profile

Over 30 years since arriving in Japan, Ryan Nelson has worked with major foreign providers of treasury management solutions and other mission critical financial software to both financial institutions and corporates. His responsibilities run from multi-billion yen negotiations with CEOs and CTOs, to hands-on management of Japanese teams working in a multi-cultural environment.

Frank's Foreword

Ryan Nelson's work with major Japanese corporations and financial institutions gives him a unique perspective on the impact of culture on business. He warns that unless they move towards 21st-century thinking and processes, they will lose their best and brightest staff and suffer commercially. He believes that foreign partners and non-Japanese Japan-insider leaders have a critical role to play in achieving positive change.

Interview

FRANK: You work for a company that provides critical software to institutions globally. Compared to western markets, how does "culture" impact your business in Japan?

RYAN: In many ways, I feel that culture is holding companies back. People talk about the Japanese attitude to risk, for example. I believe that sort of thinking stems from the postwar manufacturing era when you had to make millions of components with zero defects and zero tolerance for failure. It served Japan well at the time and helped turn it into an economic powerhouse, but it had the unintended effect of creating an unhealthy culture of risk-aversion driven by an unwillingness to take responsibility for failure. This then spawned the culture of outsourcing, where typically the first company you outsource never does the work, they pass it down the line to three or four or maybe five additional companies down the chain. Doing so, they are trying to outsource risk and make money at the same time. That's clearly not a viable strategy. It does however mean that if something goes wrong there is always someone to blame.

I think it goes back to that mentality of *ishi no ue ni mo san nen* (bide your time and be patient) combined with a practice of delegating risk to *shitauke* (preferred vendors). Culture gets in the way of business too much. If you can't take risks, how do you challenge and come up with new ideas? How do you grow?

And more importantly, how do you keep your best and brightest staff? I was having dinner recently next to a table of ten or so young people, 25 or 26-year-olds. I don't know what company they worked for, but they were obviously having a work drinks party. They were quizzing one guy who had recently quit. They were all great friends and everyone was praising him as a great co-worker, asking "Why are you quitting? You're really good." He finally spoke up and said, "I just can't stand the bullshit. I couldn't be bothered. I'm sorry, I know you're still working there, but I just can't deal with the bosses. There's just no imagination." This is the dilemma: companies are losing their best talent because of the no-risk culture.

FRANK: How do you think us Japan-insider foreigners can help tackle these challenges?

RYAN: I've often thought that foreign companies, through joint ventures, could be a bigger part of the solution. Successful joint ventures between Japanese and foreign companies are few and far between in Japan, but, if done properly, they may offer a new way to help Japanese companies take some risk and not just outsource it. Western business culture is better at engaging talented employees and might help some Japanese companies.

FRANK: What do you think is the core challenge for Japanese banks and financial institutions?

RYAN: They know they have to do something, but they face the same challenge as big companies everywhere: their complex structures seriously limit their ability to change. Politics, personal conflicts and favoritism are rife in companies everywhere, so there's nothing really unique about Japan. But there are differences. In Japan the challenges can be more complicated because the politics is often a little more subtle. In western culture it's in your face, but in Japan everything is so much more indirect. Your nemesis knows somebody who knows this other person who knows the person who matters and who went to the same University. Add to this the risk aversion and it's a mess.

A few years back, we were pitching the international team at a large Japanese financial institution on how we could help them with some challenging international payment issues. Talks went on for several months where we eventually reached an agreement and signed a contract. Then, just one month after signing the contract, a major organizational change was announced which completely restructured the international payments division. We were like... WTF? And to add insult to injury, the key people we were working with were reassigned to unrelated departments. They completely pulled the rug out from under the entire project. Everybody who knew anything was sent away. We were dumbfounded, like, "What just happened? How can they do this?" It was a significant project at $80 million. The instruction was, "OK, let's start again." It took a good eight months to get back on track, and, as far as we could see, was fueled purely by internal politics, not for any obvious business reason. We were pretty lucky to recover from that one!

And I don't think these issues are unique to large organizations. The smaller players hire people from the larger organizations. It's the exact same guys moving around. The problem isn't the people themselves. They are usually the smarter more progressive ones. The problem is the company culture and the senior people. They are stumbling through life. They don't know how to run projects. They don't really know what they want to do. One day they're worried about functions, the next day they're worried about costs, then they're worried about risk. They are just all over the place. I don't see any major difference with the smaller guys.

And the situation is even worse in the regional banks. I was in a bank recently and they showed me their operational process which of course was still paper-based. There were two printers with different colored paper, one for requests, and another for responses. That's the level of sophistication. They have a big stack of toner cartridges, and a big stack of paper, and a person in charge of changing the paper and toner. Some of them are still using dot matrix printers!

We will see a consolidation of the regional banks in Japan. There's no doubt about it. They served a purpose during a certain period, but no longer. Some will simply go out of business, others will merge. Net banks, and Seven-Eleven, will take over a lot of what the regionals used to do.

Covid has accelerated some change in business culture. People have got a taste for work-life balance and many will resist going back to a three-hour daily commute to the office. That's a given. Initially, there was a big panic about how to enable people to work efficiently from home. Buying laptops, addressing security and communication issues, etc. But all of that basic stuff has evolved really well. All the technology around security and processes, and your ability to have secure access to information anywhere, that's all definitely here to stay.

But I think there still an awful lot of resistance on the part of companies and other institutions to improving fundamental business processes. Too many senior people don't even see why they need to change, let alone know how to make it happen. We need mavericks willing to take a risk; they do exist but are few and far between.

FRANK: So, how do you deal with that?

RYAN: You have to figure out how to get clients to help themselves. Sometimes this is by lobbying the industry through things like transparency of process, shared KPIs, and proper risk management. Sometimes it's by collaborative problem-solving by sharing risk and even cost across specific segments or clients in specific locations.

Transparency is a great tool. If you can achieve transparency, you can drive improvements. A good example is the delivery process for the likes of Japan Post, Amazon, Rakuten, Kuroneko etc. The end user can see, compare and contrast the delivery services of each. This drives a healthy desire within the companies to optimize their processes, no one wants the embarrassing title of "The Slowest and Most Costly Service." Doing this locally is good, but at the global level is great!

Many Japanese companies have finally retired the old-fashioned "stamp rally" process, moved on from the piles of printouts, and modernized their operations. But would they have done this without out the catalyst of transparency? Probably not, at least nowhere as quickly as this has evolved.

FRANK: That's a great example of using *gaiatsu* (applying pressure from the outside), rather than just trying to resolve things within Japan only. Do you think this approach can work elsewhere?

RYAN: Used selectively, yes I do. The next area where I think we may be able to affect positive change in Japan is climate change action. At a recent regional meeting I would say that half of the presentations and discussions were about climate change. I was pleasantly shocked by how serious the financial sector is taking this. They're talking about making loans more expensive and harder to get for non-green or non-carbon neutral companies. Some banks won't even work on IPOs with companies unless they are carbon-neutral. There is huge pressure and it's increasing. It's a great example of a global engineered approach that is going to lift a lot of industries to a higher level. And I think there's going to be a huge opportunity there. The effort that the banks and the financial industry as a whole are putting into this is substantial. I've heard that 80% of their focus is on this. Japan has always been a bit slow to go green and carbon-neutral, but I think that will accelerate as well.

FRANK: Moving to a different topic: team management. You have over 20 years of experience managing Japanese teams, and I know it is something you enjoy and are very good at. But, even for you, are there issues that still challenge you today?

RYAN: I'm sometimes broadsided by some very different cultural perceptions regarding job responsibility. Some time back I had one guy, early-to-mid forties. He'd been with us for about two years, and had been consistently missing deadlines. We'd had several discussions over 18 months or so. It got to the stage where he missed a very important deadline, causing a lot of grief to different departments internally and also to the client. He actually knew and acknowledged that he had an issue. So I just said to him, "What can I do to help you fix this?" And he shocked me by his response. He said, "Oh! Is it that important?" And I said, "What do you mean?" To which he replied, "You never threatened me or said you'd to reduce my salary or that I'd be fired if I didn't meet my deadlines."

Well, I'm going... "That's not really how I manage people. I tend to find that the carrot works better than the stick. But you're telling me that you need the stick?" It really threw me off. I'd been talking to this guy for two years, and I've been explaining to him why it's important, and I've been explaining the impact he's having on others. I'm trying to talk to him like a normal guy, without coming on and saying, "I'm gonna fire you if you don't make this deadline." And I asked him, "Does it help you if I tell you that?" And he said, "Yes." It got me to thinking, how many other people are like this in the company!

We had done personality assessments of the team, so I went back and looked at his profile. I realized I should have read it earlier. I should have really honed in on his personality to find how to better manage him. That said, there is a limit! Especially in Japan when everything is so indirect, the more people you have involved in a process, the more chaos and uncertainty can be introduced by the multiple different personalities, and objectives, and goals and hidden agendas. Sometimes I'm amazed that anything gets done at all! And then you have an earthquake, or a typhoon or a tidal wave. There's no question about it, managing people in Japan can indeed be a huge challenge, even for us bilingual, multi-cultural foreigners!

11
- Tom Perry -

"The ideal situation is to have a Japan-insider foreigner as Country Manager supported by a strong Japanese 2IC. This way you can leverage the strengths of both people - the cultural bridging role of the Japan-insider, and the deep local knowledge and expertise of the Japanese 2IC."

Profile

Tom Perry has worked in media management in Japan for almost 30 years. He began in the home entertainment industry with CIC Video (Universal and Paramount Pictures), before moving to the then nascent digital satellite TV business as a member of the team responsible for launching DirecTV Japan. Tom later moved to the channel side of the business as Japan Country Manager of Discovery Channel and Animal Planet. He then joined Warner Media-owned Turner Japan, first running Cartoon Network Japan, then, through an M&A deal, MondoTV and Tabi Channel, and finally adding CNN Japan. In the process, his company become the largest foreign-owned producer of TV programming in the market. Tom specializes in marketing, TV programming and production, new business development, sales, licensing, M&A integration, and in building, reorganizing and managing teams. He is fluent in speaking and reading Japanese.

Frank's Foreword

Tom and I were founding members of the Japanese digital cable and satellite business. While I subsequently moved on to a different industry, Tom continued to work in the same industry for his entire career as Japan Country Manager for two major US-owned media groups. I was particularly interested in his thoughts on the cultural aspects of engaging local staff, getting the best out of your leadership team, and working with head office through the prism of his industry.

Interview

FRANK: If you were asked tomorrow to take on a new Japan Country Manager position, how would you structure the leadership?

TOM: It really differs depending on whether it's a startup, or an already established business. If it's a startup, the ideal is to have a three-person team. You need a Japan-insider foreigner who can give you an "in Japan but not of Japan" perspective. You need a bilingual Japanese executive who can offer a deeper local perspective. And you need a head office person who understands everything at that end and has all the necessary connections. If you can get these three people working together to launch your new business, you can be sure you'll have robust and well-communicated launch and growth strategies. In time, the head office person should hand the reins to the Japan-insider but continue to support Japan from outside.

If you already have an established business in Japan, then it really doesn't make any sense to have a head office person on the ground in Japan. For established companies, the extravagance of the old-style expats is a thing of the past. You should already have all the head office expertise filtering in through your various divisions. What you need on the ground is local knowledge and not just another person from the head office. The ideal situation is to have a Japan-insider foreigner as Country Manager supported by a strong Japanese 2IC. This way you can leverage the strengths of both people - the cultural bridging role of the Japan-insider, and the deep local knowledge and expertise of the Japanese 2IC.

FRANK: What are some of the common mistakes you've seen made by foreign companies in Japan?

TOM: Something I've run into several times over my career is head office trying to impose a one-size-fits-all global strategy in Japan. For example, the way they handle contracts. So many times, I've seen foreign companies insist that their Japanese partners or customers sign a 100-page English contract. The truth is that most Japanese customers won't even have anybody in-house that can read English. Insisting that they do sign it creates a huge level of misunderstanding and potential ill will right from the get-go.

As the Japan-insider foreigner, I have spent so much time trying to convince head office people that if they want to increase the number of customers and have happier customers, they've got to come up with a Japanese contract or a mutually acceptable solution. Western-style contracts may have worked for bigger, more powerful US companies in the past, but now, if you want to go beyond the top layer of Japanese customers like the big trading companies, you are really making life hard for yourself. And when a Japanese company does sign, it's because they don't care. They'll just sign whatever anyway because they know they're protected under Japanese law.

At one company I inherited a "contract standoff" when I joined. My employer was insisting on using a massive English contract and the Japanese partner was insisting on a massive Japanese contract. Both sides were insisting that, in the event of conflict, their version be legally binding. In the end, they agreed to sign both versions, and deal with the conflict issue if and when it ever came up.

Compounding the above problems is that local Japanese staff will often not push back and fight their case. Even if they speak English, they may be intimidated by the head office people, or be so happy to be in a foreign firm that they feel it's their job is to evangelize foreign culture and business practices. Whatever the reason, the result is that they passively accept orders from above, even though they know themselves that implementing them will be impossible. I remember a case where an important Japanese customer was very unhappy about having to comply with some very unreasonable requirements from our regional office in Singapore. I checked with my Japanese account manager, and sure enough he had passed on an obviously impossible demand from Singapore which seriously upset the Japanese customer. His only explanation was, "Well, they asked me to do it. How can I say no?"

FRANK: I totally agree. This is a huge issue in the character and brand-licensing business. I remember several years ago when I was running the Japanese office for a UK-based kids' brand, we had a master licensee sitting between us and about 100 smaller local sub-licensees. The head contract with the master licensee was in English, which was fine because they were a large international company. But there was no way the sub-licensees could deal with an English contract. I was amazed to find, however, that head office had been insisting that the master licensee issue contracts in English to the sublicensees. It was crazy! We eventually came up with a mutually acceptable solution by splitting the contract into a boiler-plate section and a "variable-terms" section. I had the boiler plate translated (and shortened as much as possible) into Japanese and certified by an international law firm, so that never changed. The two-page "variable-terms" section was bilingual and captured all the customer-specific information and any special conditions. It worked very well, and I used the same model at subsequent companies too.

TOM: In most cases my solution has been to just grind it out with the international people and stand my ground until we had created a Japan-appropriate contract that was as brief as possible. Obviously, the ideal would be to have an in-house, bilingual Japanese lawyer, but the most realistic option that I have found is to use a local outside law firm that is capable of communicating with our head office.

FRANK: How have you managed the cross-cultural communication challenge?

TOM: You always have to be monitoring communications between head office, your team, and your local customers. Sometimes it's a language issue, but usually it's due to culture and very different communication styles. Often, the Japanese side wants to avoid telling the foreign side that something is impossible, so it's just easier for them to say "yes" and hope it won't turn into a big problem.

But as the local leader, you can't get in the middle of everything. If you're not careful, you end up micromanaging, and that doesn't work for sure. It's almost like you're a doctor, or a plumber. You get called in when something isn't flowing the way it should be, and before the pipe blows up. You must figure out what's happening on both sides and fix the cause - which is usually communication - not just the symptoms.

FRANK: You've reminded me of a situation in the early days of satellite TV in Japan. We were launching our very first channel, which was coming into Japan from our regional office in Hong Kong via a recently launched satellite. We were supposed to be allocated a Ku-Band (frequency) transponder. This was very important because this was the designated frequency for broadcast in Japan. Right before our channel launch, we were told by Hong Kong that we had to use a C-Band transponder which, without getting into detail, was a massive technological challenge in Japan. This created huge problems for our Japanese cable operators and seriously compromised local trust and relationships. In retrospect, we should have just pushed back and simply refused to launch unless we got a Ku-Band transponder. But, even with foreigners involved, the mood in Japan was to accept the head office decision and just make it work. Luckily, another Japanese partner came to the rescue and we averted potential disaster.

TOM: I believe you need both bilingual foreigners and bilingual Japanese on your leadership team to be really effective. The cultural gap - and the way the language is used on both sides - is so different that you need both. I've had many instances where I will be in important negotiations in Japanese, but I will double check that I've understood everything with a trusted Japanese colleague. And the reverse happens too where, for example, I'll be on a head office management call with my Japanese CFO and he will check with me after the call.

There are rare exceptions of totally bilingual and bicultural people, both Japanese and foreigners. But in most cases even when people claim to be bilingual, they are 100% in their own language, and, if they're really good, they're probably 80% in the other language. So, it's always good to work in tandem with your Japanese colleagues. It's a partnership.

A typical scenario is where your company is rolling out some global project and they'll tell me (the Japan Country Manager) that I don't need to get involved. They say they have good communication with your IT people, and it's going to be fine. Then, of course, I only hear about it when there's very little time left and realize that the whole thing is totally not appropriate for the Japanese market. And I'll only hear about it when the local vendor goes nuts because it's against Japanese specs, or procedures or technical requirements. It wasn't either side trying to deceive the other side. It just an entirely different approach to project management and communication. On the foreign side, there's typically an assumption that, OK, we know Japan is a little bit different, and a little bit harder than other places in Asia, but it works everywhere else, so it'll all work out. And because they know Japan would be difficult, they've left it to last and so have no option but to force it through. And then you have real fireworks here because the technical ecosystem is so often very different in Japan.

I'll give you one example from my time at DirecTV. We were in the planning stages of launching a billion-dollar platform. The finance department in the planning company was staffed by expats from Hughes Electronics and a Japanese team from our main partner, Mitsubishi. I was sitting on the Japanese side as a member of the program team. It was quite a complex business model because of the structure of the pay-TV industry in Japan, and covered everything from revenue and cost projections, channel packages, revenue allocations by channel, the licensing structure, and the like. We were using the Japanese version of Microsoft Excel and the Hughes guys were using the English version. We were working for six to eight months on these giant spreadsheets that were being copied back and forth between the English and Japanese versions.

Then at a crucial point when we were about to go operational, one of the Hughes guys told me there was something strange happening with the model. He said every that time they hit recalculate, all the numbers in the model randomly changed. These were big numbers, really big numbers! It turned out it was an Excel bug between the Japanese version of Excel and the English version. This was in 1995 or 1996 so Microsoft had already been in Japan a long time with huge companies using their software. I guess the challenges of our business model was the first one complicated enough to initiate the bug! Microsoft has since fixed this bug, but at the time any changes to the Japanese spreadsheets had to be literally hand inputted into the English Excel sheet because of the virus problem. Thanks Microsoft!

A valuable lesson I learned from this experience is to never be the first customer for a foreign software program rollout in Japan. In addition to the usual risks you'll encounter in any country, the additional challenge in Japan is the highly segmented ecosystem with multiple vendors and software involved in any one project. Microsoft might have fixed the Excel issue, but similar issues still happen today on big overseas-initiated projects. So, you end up with complicated and expensive workarounds, like a bespoke upgrade to the Japanese version, or getting in even more vendors! Or even worse, your global vendor will bring in Japanese subcontractors that they may not even have worked with before. Ultimately, as the guinea pig, you end up doing their work for them in debugging the Japanese version, and in the meantime have seriously upset your Japanese customers and vendors and have created serious stress for your staff.

My default position on international IT projects is that if the software company does not have an established office in Japan with Japanese software engineers and proven products, then they shouldn't even be considered. And, if I'm going to be forced to implement the software anyway, then you must recognize that we're providing a service in debugging their product for Japan, and we should be incentivized and resourced accordingly.

FRANK: You mentioned that problems are often caused by entirely different approaches to business, like on the DirecTV launch project. Do you have any other examples of differences in thinking?

TOM: One fundamental difference between Japanese and western companies is the thinking around "market share" and "profitability." I've had more than one experience of joining a joint venture being run by the Japanese partner that was operating on very thin margins, sometimes breakeven. Then, at some point, growth peters out, and the Japanese side doesn't know how to fix the situation. The foreign side decides they need to take control, and that's where I came in.

The underlying issue is that many Japanese companies focus on market share, not profitability. There's nobody in the organization in Japan telling them otherwise, or even considering alternatives. I've seen it several times where there are multi-million dollar deals with just a 1% profit margin built into the contract. There can be many reasons, but it is often because they're trying to prop up some customer or keep a content production pipeline going when it's clearly not working. This is very different from foreign companies who don't want revenue growth if it means that profit margins are decimated. It is very common that the first time the Japanese staff, at all levels and business functions, are ever asked about the profitability of their deals or ROI is when the foreign partner gets more involved.

FRANK: How did you deal with these situations?

TOM: What I learned very quickly was that it is critical to have transparency and openness on numbers across the entire business. This is often about demolishing silos. In extreme cases you get the marketing people, for example, saying, "Well if I don't spend it, I'm going to lose it. So, I'm just going to go ahead and spend it like I always do every year!" I remember one situation where the print-marketing team were blatantly over-spending, rather than sharing some of that budget with digital marketing which would clearly have been more effective.

Across-the-board transparency with numbers is critical, not just between the GM and the CFO, but at the very least with all your leadership team who must also understand revenue growth and profitability growth goals. And they must be open to some tough discussions sometimes. So, maybe marketing does need to cut a few things, or they can't buy as many premium goods this year as they bought last year because money would be more effectively used elsewhere. Or maybe their time would be best used on a creative campaign to use up premium goods in the warehouse rather than just write them off as dead inventory. Stuff like that.

When you walk into a distressed business with a brief to turn it around, there are often some simple, logical things that can be done that can make a big difference. Like getting people to focus on key financial KPIs, to understand the big picture, find new customers, adapt the product, scrutinize costs, and just have honest discussions on how to make more money.

The endgame is about achieving sustained change in the way the team thinks, and in the business culture. For me, the first step in changing minds is to open up to them through transparency on the numbers and goals. I've been shocked by how often that hadn't been done. All the marketing person knew was what their own budget was, and the same for the programming person. And not only that, but they also don't want to know more, because it might mean having to make some compromises with colleagues from other departments. The salesperson doesn't want to know about profitability. He/she just has a sales target to meet, otherwise they won't get their bonus.

After transparency, the next thing is to engage the full team in building the new plan. It takes time, but you must have a working plan that involves everyone and is supported by everyone from the beginning. An important role for the foreign General Manager is to come up with outside-the-box new ideas and approaches to engage everyone in that process. I find off-site events very effective. Get people out of the normal conference room and brainstorm with whiteboards and the like to encourage new thinking. As much as possible, I try to create a sense of equality - all ideas are valid, everyone can input in the plan.

Having everyone understand the plan also helps in the event that you need to make major changes or take tough decisions. If staff have been engaged from the outset, people tend to accept the situation.

The traditional Japanese company is a kind of pyramid built from self-contained black boxes. The salespeople have total control over anything that went on inside the sales department, and so on. Departmental decisions are made without reference to the bigger picture, or even to a directly related department. For example, I had a case where adverting sales, marketing, and cable sales teams were ordering video production from external, and more expensive, production companies rather than use our internal production department. Part of the reason for that was that our production team, for some reason, refused to work from a brief from their internal client. So, you end up with the sales and marketing teams coming up with these expensive work-arounds rather than addressing the core problem.

And compounding the smaller problems is that, typically, no one in senior management is interested in fixing the larger problems. You end up with an organization where people either just do what they want, or they're treating it like a hobby rather than a serious job. My solution was to build a culture of transparency and logic, but this is actually a very common problem at Japanese companies generally, with an incredible cost to the economy.

FRANK: You talked about the importance of transparency, and engaging the team in the development of the plan. But what if you have someone, and especially someone senior, who won't get on board, and is even disruptive. How do you deal with that?

TOM: Well, if you've got one person who thinks they're so indispensable that they don't have to follow this new plan that everybody, including yourself, has put together, the truth is that they are more destructive by staying. You've got to encourage them to quit, no matter how painful that might be for you and the company in the short term. I've had this experience, and, in many cases, such people are so adamant about their opposition they will quit on principle.

FRANK: Tell me about your experiences dealing with your overseas boss.

TOM: The best boss I can think of hired me to take over the operation in Japan and told me just two things. "Firstly," he said, "I don't know anything about Japan... that's why I hired you! But secondly, I expect you to make your numbers." And I was like, this is awesome. That was the first time I'd had a boss overseas say anything like that to me. But of course, being a foreign company, he moved on at some point. In that particular entity, where I spent 15 years, he was one of seven bosses I had, so an average of about 2.2 years per boss.

But I've had a few bad bosses too. When I say "bad," I mean that they didn't understand Japan, maybe even disliked Japan, but had strong ideas anyway. This has been even more difficult with Covid because you can't get them here physically to give them as much transparency as possible by visiting key customers, key vendors, and the like. The toughest cases are when they just won't listen at all. Despite your best advice they insist on - and even get aggressive about - doing something their way. So sometimes you just have to let them fail. Just step out of the way and then try to save them from the situation three months, six months down the road. It's obviously not good to have that happen, but if there's no other way they can learn, what else can you do!

And that happens a lot because your Japanese customers, and others in the market, are not going to tell you either. Maybe when you're near crisis point someone leans over and says, "What the hell are you doing?" When I was at DirecTV, I did an exclusive deal with Nickelodeon to launch in Japan. My counterpart at Nickelodeon was a decent person and negotiations went quite well. Soon after the deal was done, that person disappeared and was replaced by a team from New York. This was 1997, maybe 1998, when Nickelodeon was top of the world. They arrived in Japan with the attitude of "We're Nickelodeon, everything we touch turns into solid gold. We've done this in hundreds of countries across the world before Japan, so just stay out of our way." Such was the level of hubris, they were insisting, for example, on a totally unpronounceable version of the channel name in Japanese.

They refused to adapt in any way to suit the needs of the Japanese market and just kept bashing everybody in Japan who tried to advise them otherwise. Things came to a head when JCOM management was so furious after one meeting that not only were they threatening to drop Nickelodeon, but its sister-channel MTV too. Japanese buyers just don't want to deal with such arrogance. And why should they! There are plenty of other kids' channels, and other music channels too.

Nickelodeon is no longer in Japan, which, I think, says it all!

12
- Paul Riley -

"Head Office said the failure rate at 3% was acceptable by global standards and instructed us to ship the product. We pushed back and explained that the standard in Japan is 0%."

Profile

Paul Riley began his 35-year-long career in language education as a teacher, before joining Isuzu Motors Ltd. in 1992 where he was responsible for all training exchanges among Isuzu Motors and their overseas partners and international subsidiaries. In 1997 he began a 22-year career in English Language Learning with Oxford University Press (OUP), joining as a sales rep and rising to Japan Country Manager in just three years. Paul continued to climb the ranks at OUP in a series of regional and global roles including Director, ELT Channels and Partnerships. In 2017 he moved to his current company, World Family English - a leading provider of English language learning products and services primarily for children aged 0 to 7 - as Vice President, Innovation and Global Services. His recent professional focus is on the development and delivery of mobile educational content, and the commercialization of new initiatives in emerging areas of educational technology.

Frank's Foreword

Paul Riley has worked at the forefront of sales and marketing for most of his 35-year career in Japan. I was interested in both his Japan Country Management experience at OUP - which was one of the biggest ELL publishers at the time - and his fascinating role at the forefront of consumer sales and marketing at World Family English.

Interview

FRANK: World Family is one of the biggest and most successful foreign-founded direct-sales companies in Japan. Can you tell us a little about the company's history?

PAUL: The predecessor company was selling English-language encyclopedias in Asia in the 1960s. The then CEO, a man named David Smith, realized that the real opportunity for English was in self-study language learning materials. He partnered with a linguist at Harvard University and they created their first course, targeting adult learners. They brought the business to Japan in the 1970s at a time when people were finding themselves with some disposable income and were thinking about overseas travel. The initial business was a travel membership scheme that helped people prepare their arrangements, not just the language but also visa applications and other pre-travel preparation. Following the success of its adult program, the company then published a similar self-study learning product for children, featuring characters from the Walt Disney Company, which was named *Disney's World of English.* This was 1978, about the time that construction of Tokyo Disneyland started. They predicted that the opening of the park (which happened in 1983) would drive the popularity of Disney characters and the brand in Japan.

The fact that (the now named) *Disney World of English* is still the market leader in pre-school English education in Japan (and East Asia) suggests they were right.

FRANK: It almost seems too easy! But what do you think underlies your brand's popularity with Japanese consumers?

PAUL: I think there are several things. Of course, the brand is important. The product definitely benefited from the publicity created by Tokyo Disneyland. But timing was important too. We were first-to-market in Japan with this kind of product and were able to capture market share very early. This also underpins our longevity in the market. The early-adopters 40 years ago are now grandparents, and have quite likely recommended our courses to the two generations that followed. Another factor is the attention we pay to customer service and the customer experience. We offer a full warranty on the product. We have large call centers in all markets that will answer customers' questions seven days a week. That's a huge investment in infrastructure, but it means that our customers are very loyal and almost evangelical.

Our hiring policy is also important. We look for mothers who have used the product with their children and are ready to rejoin the labor market. They know the product firsthand and can talk to customers with authenticity. I would estimate that up to 80% of our salespeople are former customers or mothers, and this has created a virtuous circle of user-to-employee. With that comes the word-of-mouth publicity through real stories about their own experiences with their children. Instead of professional sales, it's very homey. We recruit some professional salespeople, but for the most part they are inexperienced parents who learn on the job.

But at the end of the day, the product must work, and it is our proven track record in generating fluency outcomes that drives the business today. With language learning there is no magic bullet. It requires commitment, thousands of hours! Most children start from 0~2 years old, so they don't have much agency. So the mother must be committed and motivated. A lot of this comes from our community of like-minded people.

FRANK: You mentioned motivation. Japan is notorious for not being motivated to learn English. And why should they! I faced this with my own daughter. From her perspective, everything in her world works in Japanese, so why should she learn another language! But you seem to have achieved a much higher level of engagement with your product than competing products have.

PAUL: It's easy to put it down to the popularity of Disney characters, but I think the real difference is that we start earlier and at a critical period when language learning is most effective. Research has shown that any child can learn a language in the right conditions and at the right age. What we've tried to do is mimic those conditions where you've got a lot of input but low pressure to produce, so it's a more natural and fun approach to learning. It's akin to immersion, but it's not. It's an artificial bubble encapsulating the mother and child at home or in the child's room, and it allows a lot more meaningful connection to the language than you would get in a traditional setting. If you go to an *eikaiwa* (English language school) you'll only get an hour a day, or a couple of hours a week. But research has shown that you need 2,000~3,000 hours to achieve a decent competency level. So our goal is to facilitate that level of exposure in the home. That's not easy! There are so many distractions - soccer practice, piano practice, *juku* (cram school), but by starting early we are able to establish ourselves in the lifestyle of both the children and their parents.

For us, it's all about communicative competence and having fun; not standardized tests or entrance exam prep. We also focus on teaching positive and motivational values such as sharing, being kind and polite, diversity, following your dreams, etc. The syllabus grows with the learner. It starts at a young age with simple developmental toys that are designed for cognitive development as well as language learning.

FRANK: How would you compare Japan to your other markets?

PAUL: Japanese users stay with our program significantly longer than people in other markets. In Japan, our average retention is about 65 months – more than five years – with most kids graduating at around ten years old. In other Asian markets they finish at about six years old and move on to cram school programs to pass standardized tests. By the end of first grade, parents want to see how well their children are progressing compared to others in international standards. Our program doesn't satisfy the real tiger moms! And that's true for Japan too. For all our success, there is a cohort that will not consider our program.

FRANK: What is your biggest challenge in terms of expanding the business?

PAUL: The biggest challenge is launching in new markets with a direct-to-consumer business model. In Japan, Taiwan and Hong Kong we have more than 30 years' experience and many of our salespeople are former users. But what do you do when you don't have an installed user base? You've got to figure out how to sell it without this cohort of mothers who will go out and do it for you. We've been in Korea since 2014 and we're only starting to build our sales team with former users now. The early years were a real challenge. Realistically we will probably have to look at different business models to expand our markets.

FRANK: One thing I've seen with kids' character licensing is that, compared to other markets, Japanese stay engaged with characters to an older age. It's not unusual to see a parent, for example, wearing a Thomas the Tank Engine or Pingu T-shirt! Is that true for your business too?

PAUL: Absolutely! We use the full universe of Disney animated characters, but our core products are based on the classic character set like Mickey, Minnie, Donald, Daisy, Goofy, Pluto, and Winnie the Pooh. In Korea, kids lose interest in these characters very quickly and move to the *Pixar* and *Frozen* market. Here in Japan, playing up the Mickey/Minnie element works really well. Girls, in particular, stay with our program into their teenage years and don't see anything wrong with it. I think having the theme park in Japan makes a huge difference.

FRANK: What is the most important thing you've learned about Japanese consumers?

PAUL: The need to deliver perfection out of the box! I've seen this time and time again over my career in Japan. If you are selling a premium product, it must look and feel "premium" and be supported by premium customer service. In Korea, speed is the most important thing: "Just put it out there. It may go wrong but iterate and get it right!" Most of the trends there grow very quickly and the consumer cycles are very fast, so success is often tied to speed to market. If you miss the boat, you'll never catch up. In Japan, everything is a slow burn. And once you get into a market and you establish your credentials, you tend to be in there for a long time.

I think this is related to a feeling of respect that Japanese people have for heritage brands. Years ago, when I was with Oxford University Press (OUP), we were planning a marketing campaign to celebrate the 25th anniversary of one of our best-selling courses. Everybody in Japan was very enthusiastic, but Korea said, "No. 25 years just says that you're old. That's not the message we want to give people." But in Japan it's comforting and denotes something you can trust.

This creates opportunities for heritage brands like OUP. We dominated the hand-held electronic dictionary market in Japanese high schools, for example, because we were recognized as the genuine dictionary brand. This happens a lot in Japan, where certain items become the standard, and are passed down from generation to generation. Unlike Korean consumers who are always looking for the next thing, in Japan, there isn't this overwhelming desire or need to change. It's a very different mindset.

Consistency in product presentation and customer service is also critical. When I was at Oxford, we had always done our quality control and packaging in Japan. Then we received a directive from head office to switch it to China where the cost was a quarter of the cost in Japan. We had our misgivings, but had no choice but to comply. When the first shipment came in for one of our biggest customers, it was a mess, at least by Japanese standards. There were items packaged in the wrong order, the shrink-wrap was loose and even covers were bent or torn. Head office said the failure rate at 3% was acceptable by global standards and instructed us to ship the product. We pushed back and explained that the standard in Japan is 0%. Ultimately, of course, the customer refused to take the shipment and we reverted to doing quality control in Japan at the higher cost.

I've encountered this several times over the years. What I've usually done is take a cost-cutter from head office to experience customer service in Japan themselves. And I don't mean a high-class restaurant where you're paying for high-quality service. I mean a gas station where a uniformed attendant on minimum wage bows and cleans your windscreen. That's the service expectation in Japan. So, if you are going to put your brand on a product or service and call it "premium," it had better be perfect!

FRANK: Why is Japan wired like that?

PAUL: I think there are two things at play. One is a strong sense of community. I think it stems from the cooperative nature of the school system. Primary school, and even below, in Japan is very cooperative and inclusive. The kids eat lunch together, they serve it to each other, they clean the classrooms and hallways together, they learn about harmony and being a useful part of the community. This is all learned at an early age, and I think it sticks with them.

The other is a weak sense of "social class." Let me give you a personal example. I play tennis at a competitive level. I am accepted as part of that group because I'm a reasonably good tennis player. Nobody there knows or cares what I do for a living. One guy's a commercial fisherman, one is a taxi driver, and another is a doctor. There is no stigma attached to these jobs and for whatever reason, the Japanese seem to believe that the best thing for society is for everyone to do the best job they can in whatever they do. And people respect and appreciate that. Whereas in Ireland, or the UK or the US, if you are in an hourly-waged job, the attitude is, “I’m not paid to be polite.”

FRANK: Is this related to a strong sense of empathy? People are thinking, “What would I expect? Therefore I’ll deliver it in a way that will make me happy.”

PAUL: Yes, empathy and common purpose. Take masks, for example. In other countries, people take their masks off the first chance they get. But in Japan people will keep them on even when they are walking alone on a beach! It’s a little crazy, but it’s also comforting because it’s coming from a sense of collective purpose. It’s helped by the fact that Japan is predominantly monocultural, and without divisive ideologies or religion.

FRANK: Brands often talk about having a “secret sauce.” For Thomas and Friends, for example, it was the simple idea of putting faces on trains. What’s your secret sauce?

PAUL: Obvious answers would be that the product actually works, or our hiring policy of focusing on mothers who have actually used and loved our product. This enables us, among other things, to offer the best customer service in our industry. Our biggest competitor has a nice-looking product and spends a huge amount on marketing, but they will never match the level of customer service we offer.

But I actually think our secret sauce is our DIY ethos. We do lots of events, for example, that have a “home-made” feel to them. We deliver a high-quality experience but always with heart and warmth; not glitz and glamor like the competition tends to do. Warmth is our differentiator. I’ve also seen this elsewhere in publishing. Products may be technically proficient, but they just don't have a voice, or "warmth." It's something intangible that a formulaic program doesn't have.

FRANK: What is the most important thing for a non-Japanese Country Manager when it comes to working with Japanese partners?

PAUL: For a foreign company, the top priority with partners is relationship-building, which takes time and commitment. Head offices often don't understand this and wonder why you are not delivering results after your first six months. Things are changing. You can always go to Amazon or somewhere to get quick business, but if you want long-lasting business, you've got to put the time in to build up the relationship. You've got to spend the time in the *izakaya* (Japanese-style pub) drinking with them, get naked at an *onsen* (hot spring), and show them that you are here for the long term. You've got to show that you'll be there when they need you. If you think that's nonsense, maybe Japan is not for you!

FRANK: What's the biggest mistake foreign companies make?

PAUL: Short-term thinking. The ELL publishing industry is a perfect example. In the good old days, Japan was making money and head office didn't interfere. Then there was a period where Japan would deliver consistently and maintain profitability, but there wasn't growth. But that wasn't good enough for a lot of head office people, and they would come in to push for growth. It was common for publishers to pressure distributors to take unreasonably big orders to inflate their sales. But all this did was create warehouses full of unsold books, and eventually massive returns. The next step was to force the Japan operation to cut costs and downsize. This intensified after the bubble burst and Japan suddenly stagnated and even went backwards. Today, there are only three or four foreign publishers still active in the market, compared with 20 to 25 a couple of decades ago.

What they didn't realize is that the best strategy for a foreign ELL publisher in Japan is to be boringly and consistently profitable. Even over the last 20 years when everything has been stagnating, Japanese are still paying full price for things.

FRANK: Can you talk about your experience managing Japanese employees?

PAUL: The first thing is how much the labor market has changed over the past 20 years or so. When I first joined the Japanese publishing industry it was highly unionized, with tenure-based pay scales and promotions. People knew that in a certain number of years they'll reach a certain level of seniority and have a certain wage. When I was MD at OUP, we plotted a graph of salaries as a percentage of overheads and realized we'd be out of business in five years. I spent a lot of time offering people early retirement and trying to find various ways to avert disaster. One silver lining of the economic stagnation of the last 20 years is that Japan has become more open to performance and results-oriented compensation and promotion. There's a lot less job security, which in some ways is bad, but enables businesses to stay afloat.

But there is still a legacy of the tenure-based pay scales and promotions. There is a business theory called The Peter Principle [50] which says that when people are promoted based on their success in previous roles, eventually they reach a level where they are no longer competent because their skills don't match their new position. This phenomenon exists in Japan but, in my view, it has more to do with poor mentoring and succession planning. It's an outcome of the post-WW2 era where you had iconic entrepreneurs such as Akio Morita, who stayed in power for decades but never groomed a protege. This happened at OUP too. The first MD was hired in 1955 and served for a whopping 34 years! He successfully grew the business, but he was a one-man band making all the decisions and all the rules. Like Morita, he never trained a successor, and he created a culture of yes-men. People were never taught to think for themselves.

FRANK: I could imagine this being a big obstacle for a new Country Manager trying to manage some form of change.

PAUL: I agree. I became the *bucho* (division manager) in the ELT business when I was 31. What I saw was a lot of people avoiding taking any responsibilities. 20 different *hanko* (personal seal) on an approval document! There was no single person taking responsibility for any decisions, it was all shared. I set a goal for myself to get people to accept some individual responsibility. There were many hurdles. I'd not been in the company long at that point - about four to five years. I was managing people who were nearly twice my age and had been in the company 15 or 20 years. They looked at me like I was a snotty-nosed kid. I needed to gain their trust, so I basically spent two to three years trying to be more Japanese than the Japanese themselves. I would be the first to arrive and one of the last to leave the office. I even did a couple of executive courses to improve my communication style. I wanted to show them that I was going to work as hard as they did, and try to earn their trust, so that they would think, "this guy's not just working for his pay-check; he's going to be there with us; he's going to visit the bookshops; he's going to go to the warehouse at inventory time when it's 100 degrees in August, in February when it's zero degrees." I really tried to show that I was willing to do that.

I visited our warehouse in the UK at one point and really liked the way they shared key information with all the staff through a big graphic displayed in a shared space. It had a simple color-coded system against KPIs like the number of books shipped, the number of returns, maybe the number of injuries. Green is "good", amber is "caution" and red is "Houston, we have a problem." Managers were required to take their teams there every month so they could see how their section was performing.

Back in Japan I created a similar space in the room where we had our copying machine and the coffee machine, so people would see it. At the time, we were going through quite a bumpy period, and I needed all employees to know exactly how their team was performing and to act on any problems. Ultimately, we tried to tie bonuses and pay reviews to these metrics. I made some progress, but generally companies in Japan are very bad at implementing action-based processes.

FRANK: I had a similar experience when I was in publishing. Department heads weren't talking to each other. Everybody would put their *hanko* on the approval form, and there was no ownership of key decisions. Deciding the print run for a particular title, for example, the editorial department would set a high print run to justify their P&L. The salespeople, who ultimately had to sell the book, knew about it but, as far as they were concerned, it wasn't their decision. My equivalent of your color-coded graphic was a pipeline document that showed all the key decisions and personal ownership of them. But it wasn't all about cracking down on bad decisions, we also wanted to celebrate great work, so we took it a step further by bringing the spreadsheet to life in a physical and tactile way. We created a "hall of fame" where everyone posted up on a wall what they were doing, and had a monthly "show-and-tell" where whoever was responsible got up and talked about it. Not the boss, or the *bucho*, but whoever actually did the work. I was trying to create a feeling of transparency, responsibility and also recognition for great work.

PAUL: We did a similar "key-decision ownership" document with photos of the owners. That was very effective.

Also, I found that making sure everyone knew how they were contributing to the business was very important. If you were in customer service and you saw a green light next to that metric, you're going to feel more positive and engaged. And everyone could see how they fitted into the larger puzzle. Putting this information out in a public forum where people could see it certainly helped. The social pressure to contribute positively, and not be a drag on everyone else, really helped propel teamwork.

We also used to socialize as a group, sometimes tied into an off-site session. Cross-functional activities were very effective, like a scavenger hunt with ten questions that can only be answered by talking to people from other teams. There would be five or six teams competing against each other. It was about finding fun ways to force people to talk to one another and to show that, to complete this thing, you all need to contribute. The first time we did it they thought it was nuts. Then after about the third or fourth time they really loved it and looked forward to it.

Another thing I introduced was a "Silly Awards" event. Everyone in the company would get an award. For the managers it was usually something self-deprecating. None of the awards cost more than a couple hundred yen. It was just trying to build a sense of fun and teamwork. I think there is a lot more value in that than just giving people a bonus. I don't believe that bonuses motivate people to work harder. They are effective in focusing people on what you want them to do, but in my experience, you're not going to get more effort. If you bonus top-line sales, people will focus on top-line sales to the exclusion of profitability. If you bonus the bottom line, they're going to look for cost-cutting. Particularly in Japan, I think people work as hard as they are going to work. You can make them work harder if they are part of a team and feel really invested in it, but I don't think money affects that much at all.

FRANK: I agree. While I was at Guinness World Records, there was a terrific person in charge of events who developed a corporate training program using Guinness World Records challenges. In one, he would have people do this cooperative group challenge firstly in their departmental groups, then in a cross-departmental group. Without fail, every time there was a better result when they mixed up the groups.

PAUL: Japan needs more of that sort of thing. Most of the corporate training is so awful, lecture-oriented, boring; and people are just sitting there thinking, "at least I don't have to go into the office today, and I can wear jeans, so that's great." But if you make it fun and engaging, people remember it. It took a long time to arrange these activities like the "scavenger hunt", but the team building and camaraderie and thinking that came out of it made it worthwhile.

FRANK: Do you have other examples of successful initiatives to encourage teamwork and engagement?

PAUL: I think it makes a big difference if you make yourself accessible to everyone. At one company, my predecessor had the proverbial "corner office." It was out of the way, so you had to make a point to go there. It even had its own exit! And there was an assistant right out front who would ask you why you wanted to see the GM. It was traditional old-school. He was a nice enough guy, but he just didn't engage with the staff. And he did not know what was going on in the company. When I took over, I wanted to be out in the *genba.* One of the first things I did was to convert the former GM's office into a meeting room for everyone. Japan works well in the collective. I think a boss should be among the people, but there is this cultural thing that the boss must have his own office. It's easy to fall into that practice too. I must admit I was tempted to go for the cushy office, but thought that it would shut me off from what was going on. You've got to be talking to people at the *genba*, talking to your customers, talking to your partners.

Another thing I tried to do was break down some of the ritualistic and formulaic way of doing things. Meetings, for example, were always scheduled for an hour regardless of the issue. Many of them hardly merited a five-minute conversation or didn't need to happen at all! But they're like gas in a vacuum, and expand to fill the available space.

FRANK: I heard a Country Manager talking recently about the importance of walking the corridors, especially in large companies. The way he created time for this was to keep the one-hour meeting scheduled, but that he would finish the meeting as soon as he could, and then use the rest of that time to go out and talk to people.

PAUL: Now that's a good use of time!

FRANK: What do you look for in your 2IC?

PAUL: I've always found that a *gaijin/nihonjin* (foreigner/Japanese) partnership is the best way to run a foreign-owned company in Japan. I've performed better when I have a Japanese 2IC where there is total trust, and we divide the work based on our respective strengths. My Japanese colleague will get deep into the weeds on local operations while I, as the foreigner, manage the relationship with head office. That's not to say I'm not part of the local team. As I said earlier, it's very important to me to be out there in the *genba* as much as possible, but in a general sense, that's how I would divide up the work. The *gaijin/nihonjin* partnership can also give you an advantage in negotiations. You might want to play "good cop, bad cop," or use the "*gaijin* card."

FRANK: Thinking back to the head office people that you have reported to, what are the attributes of a good boss and a bad boss?

PAUL: The best boss I've ever had was actually not my boss. It was my boss's boss, the head of Global ELT at Oxford when I first joined them in Japan. He really understood his role. We had around 45 employees in Japan, but only a handful would ever get to visit head office at Oxford University, so he wanted to do everything he could to make the connection with head office for the rest of the Japanese staff. Whenever he visited us in Japan, he would walk around the office and speak to every single person, shake their hand, say their name. If he were meeting them for the first time, he would ask a few questions; if he had met them before he would ask them something about their family or what they had told him the last time. He'd ask a few personal questions almost like a politician, and with everyone in that office he would make a personal connection. And he'd tell them about how much head office appreciated the hard work and the contribution of the Japan team.

That was so important and valuable to all these people who never got the opportunity to go Oxford and see the mothership.

And the bad bosses would do exactly the opposite. They would come in and never take the time to speak to anyone, except for maybe the leadership team. They'd stay at the best hotels and even complain about this and that. In some cases, it was almost colonial in the way they treated our Japanese staff. To be honest, it would have been better if they never came at all!

I think that being a great boss, especially in a cross-cultural situation, is about having that human touch. It's the ability to attract and retain the brightest people who would otherwise be snapped up by a much bigger company.

13
- Scott Smoler -

"The Head of International must understand that when employing a Country Manager, they are dealing with someone who has spent many years building a reputation in their market. If you screw up as their boss, you are causing serious damage to that person's reputation on their home ground. That's quite a heavy responsibility."

Profile

Scott Smoler is the Founder and CEO of weConnect, a leading provider of back-office services for foreign multinational companies, including market entry, expansion, and optimization of business operations in Japan. Over almost 15 years he has helped in excess of 1,000 Japan subsidiaries of foreign companies streamline their finance, payroll and tax functions, and has served as external Representative Director for over 50 such companies.

Frank's Foreword

I was very familiar with weConnect as a company providing a valuable service to many Japan subsidiaries of foreign companies. I was therefore delighted have the opportunity to interview its Founder and CEO, Scott, through a kind introduction from fellow contributor Harold Godsoe. As both a Japan Country Manager of his own company, and an advisor/consultant to over 1,000 foreign companies in Japan, Scott's perspective on what companies should look for in their Japan Country Manager was of particular interest to me.

Interview

FRANK: What are some of the challenges in hiring a Country Manager in Japan?

SCOTT: The biggest challenge for a foreign company coming into this market is finding a Country Manager who can both communicate with head office in a way that makes them feel comfortable, and with stakeholders in Japan - local staff, partners and, of course, with customers. It's such a critical hire. It can make or break the success of the venture, unless you're lucky enough to have a product that is so well-known it's unbreakable!

A common mistake when hiring a Japanese national as Country Manager is to go for the most bilingual candidate. Very often they'll soon discover that this person is more of an "English expert" and not as capable and successful in the space as they present themselves. A common red flag is that they've job-hopped a lot.

What I see a lot is that companies either hire a Japanese national as Country Manager, or they send someone from head office. They rarely look at what you're calling the "Japan-Insider" option. I think there are a lot of very capable Japan-based foreigners who both know the local market and can communicate with head office. But companies usually don't see it that way.

For the hundreds of small-scale market entrants coming in every year, the stakes are relatively small. Most of them are sales offices, and technical sales operations, hiring just a handful of staff. Software services is a great example where most of the sales are in contracts with overseas companies, so the Japanese entity just needs a few staff on the ground. It's a low-cost and relatively simple operation.

The higher risks are for larger companies in retail and B2C. It's hard to test the market before you come. A typical scenario is that they work with a distributor, and they are not getting the sales they want, and they think the distributor is at fault. Too often they discontinue the relationship and pull out without a Plan B in place, unaware that they're not going to be able to re-enter for a long while.

FRANK: There have been some examples of companies that came in, failed, went away, and came back again. Like IKEA and Carrefour, for example. They went away, re-thought their strategy, and got it right the next time.

SCOTT: If you have a unique and appealing offering that does not exist in Japan, then this is a great market. But if you're entering a category already covered by Japanese companies, Japanese consumers will almost always choose the Japanese product. So, there must be something unique or special, or with international cache. There are exceptions, but they are few and far between. Ultimately, it's about having an appealing product and the right approach.

FRANK: Do you have an example of a common mistake made by foreign companies entering Japan?

SCOTT: The biggest mistake, I believe, is when companies think they know Japan, usually based on experience in other markets in Asia, but actually they have very poor understanding of the market. The less a company assumes it knows about Japan, the more successful it is likely to be. Companies that have a healthy degree of trepidation about Japan are more likely to do their due diligence than companies that think they know it all. It's good to be humble, and to assume you'll need to adapt to market and cultural differences.

B2C companies generally come in with a more significant launch plan. The smart B2C companies realize they need significant help and will engage consultants to support their launch. Having the right support at this stage is critical, including help in finding the right Country Manager. And I think it's very hit and miss. It could be that the best consulting company for you might not have the best language skills, or ability to communicate with head office and persuade them to apply money in this way or that way. Too often this results in a breakdown of communication and head office ends up running the show. Also, it's rare for head office to give full control to a Country Manager they've just hired, so again, they get overly involved. Unless you've got someone on the Japan side - the Country Manager or the consultants - capable of steering head office in the right direction, things can turn sour quickly.

FRANK: That brings me to a question about the other key player in country management: the Head of International. What are some issues you've seen there?

SCOTT: The Head of International must understand that when employing a Country Manager, they are dealing with someone who has spent many years building a reputation in their market. If you screw up as their boss, you are causing serious damage to that person's reputation on their home ground. That's quite a heavy responsibility.

Just speaking as an observer, one issue that comes up is micro-management. This is bad in any context, but it's potentially disastrous when done across great distance and very different cultures, and when dealing with the most senior person in the local organization. Therefore, it's incumbent on head office to find a Country Manager they can trust, and therefore give them more responsibility and freedom, without requiring head office interference. That's where you need the trust. Because if you don't bind-in the Country Manager, especially if they are Japanese, they can disappear into a black box.

But it's not always the head office person's problem. There can be an expectation gap where the Country Manager views this as their kingdom, as if they are the CEO of Japan, whereas head office views them as just another member of staff. This is especially so with Japanese-national Country Managers. The culture gap is significant, because the success or failure of the launch depends on convincing head office one way or the other. And the communication style is so different that there is a danger of massive miscommunication.

As a back-office vendor, we often find ourselves in a mediation role. Sometimes head office doesn't talk to the Japan staff and leaves them out of the loop. So, we find ourselves in the middle of a communication gap and have to ask the head office to talk to its local staff. Left unaddressed this can lead to an ever-widening chasm between head office and Japan. A Japan-Insider Country Manager can be crucial in these situations because of having a foot in both camps.

I think that there are three types of Japanese-national Country Managers. One is the insular, old-school type who looks at the Japan business as their private fiefdom and thinks head office shouldn't be involved at all. They can be very unpleasant to work with, especially for the vendor who gets stuck in the middle when things go wrong! Then there is the seasoned professional who maybe has been a Country Manager for many different multinational companies. They know how to play the game and are very skillful in keeping head office at bay. Then there is the hidden gem: a truly internationalized professional who can work well with head office and is capable of doing the job locally.

The best Japanese-national Country Manager candidates often come from the second or third level in the best domestic companies. They could have been working for 20 years at a major player in Japan, they happen to speak good English, but they haven't done the whole international thing yet. They are attracted to your company because they really love your brand. But they are very hard to find because they are deeply hidden in domestic companies, are not actively looking for jobs, so they are not on the recruiters' radars.

FRANK: On more than one occasion when I took over as Country Manager, I found the focus wasn't on strategy. It was on process and deadlines, and contracts and discounts and all that side. I've had to shift focus to the customer and make sure the product is right for that customer. I've also heard similar comments from other Country Managers. Is this something you have experienced?

SCOTT: That's why in those situations, I think that a foreign Country Manager is often in a better position to right the ship. Probably the companies you are describing are floundering or stagnant somewhat in their local offices, so they are trying to make things incrementally better, but it's not going to be better by multiples. Because you know that they already had their shot at a marketing strategy, and they are not willing to invest significantly in Japan, so you're just trying to do incremental improvements with the resources that you have.

FRANK: So, what do you do as a company if you've hired the wrong person? You've taken on somebody who impressed you at the interview, but ultimately can't do the job. Where do you go then?

SCOTT: You must replace them at some point, and that's not an easy process. Employment laws are strong in Japan and foreign companies must be aware of how things work. We've seen some horror stories where head office tried to terminate someone in Japan as they would at home, and that has come back to bite them big time. We had one client who realized almost immediately that they had made the wrong Country Manager appointment. The person sued them for one year of salary, even though the Japan operation hadn't even launched! In this case the employee had job-hopped a lot in the past, and accepted a year's severance. But in other cases, it can cost the employer significantly more, and be very disruptive to your rollout, including bad media coverage.

But you can also see where the employee is coming from in these situations. They have taken a huge risk quitting their safe job with a Japanese company and could find it extremely difficult to find their next opportunity.

This is why I think the onboarding process is very important. For companies setting up in Japan for the first time, I always stress the importance of sending someone from head office for at least a year. They'll be making personal connections, which are more important in Japan than elsewhere. This will all help them make a better decision when hiring the Country Manager.

FRANK: What are some of the contractual issues companies and potential Country Managers should be aware of?

SCOTT: The main issue is that if you are a Representative Director, the position is at the pleasure of the board, which effectively might just mean your boss. It is difficult to fire someone within their contract term, but when that ends, labor law doesn't apply because they are not an employee. In these instances, it is relatively easy for the company to terminate the Country Manager's appointment. Many Japanese nationals insist that they be Representative Director, because otherwise they think they won't be taken seriously. It does carry a lot of power because they have the ability to bind the company into contracts, with or without the company seal.

FRANK: So, what do you think is the best option for a Country Manager: a Japanese national, or a Japan-Insider foreigner?

SCOTT: I think it's about creating a team that ensures you have both deep insights into the Japanese market, but also a strong and healthy relationship with head office. Personally, I will never understand the motivations of the Japanese consumer as well as a

Japanese person will, but then I do have the advantage of having a foot in both Japan and head office's camps. So ultimately, I think it's a "two-in-a-box" partnership between a Japan-Insider foreigner and a Japanese national. Whether it's the foreigner as the Country Manager and the Japanese as No. 2, or the other way around, it doesn't matter. The important thing is that they are aligned and working well together. There will be crossover where both people will be effective, but the foreigner's primary role is to manage head office, and the Japanese person's role is to be deep into the local business. It's got to be a team effort, including the head office-based Head of International. If any one of these players is not there, the magic won't work!

I'm a believer in matching cultures. In my company, we always have native speakers lead discussions. If we are having a conversation with a Japanese counterpart, we will have a Japanese person front the meeting from our side. I am never going to be the person trying to talk about anything of importance with a Japanese speaker in Japan. Likewise, if it's a conversation with an American counterpart, I or another native English speaker would take the lead. That's just my philosophy.

FRANK: I agree with what you said about "two-in-a-box". When I look back on my own career, I have been most effective when I've had a strong Japanese 2IC. I've also had the opposite experience on one occasion with a legacy 2IC, and it basically cost me my job. But that's a story for another day.

What's your advice on working with distributors?

SCOTT: Companies often make the mistake of either going all-in on the distributor, or all-in by themselves. Usually, they start all-in on the distributor, and when things are not working out, they to go in and take over distribution themselves. The truth is that, yes, the distributor is not prioritizing your product, but is it because the distributor is bad, or because there is an issue with your product? Most companies assume it's the former and jump to the wrong conclusion.

I think the best approach is to have a small team on the ground from day one to manage the distributor. Then you can have real insight on the true nature of any problem. I would hire the local team to help choose the distributor. That sets up the right dynamic between your team and the distributor. Doing it the other way round may cause resentment with your distributor and have your team viewed as "spies."

FRANK: I totally agree. The best way is to get your local team in first, engage them in finding the distributor, the distributor likes the local team because they were there first, and they probably prefer anyway working with a local Japanese team. I had this experience when I ran the Thomas the Tank Engine licensing business in Japan. Thanks to the foresight of a previous owner, my company, HIT Entertainment, already had a small team on the ground working very effectively with our master licensee, Sony Creative Products (SCP). We provided a valuable service to SCP, especially with quick turnaround on creative approvals, and on larger discussions with head office on major product development projects.

What do you do when head office questions whether that "extra layer" is necessary? I had this experience after a new CEO in my head office took the position that "we have a Japanese partner, and we have people in the head office who can work with the partner; so why do we need this additional layer in Tokyo?"

SCOTT: I have had similar experiences, and I am just so done in life with trying to force change in situations like that, even if I know I'm right! The reality is that you are experienced in this market, and you are working with a foreign company that is not experienced. You tell them, "This is the market reality, and you need to trust me." Either they say, "Yes," or they say, "No," but I've learned through bitter experience that trying to convince people beyond that is futile. If a company says, "No, we disagree with that, we've done this elsewhere, and this is not how we approach things and we are not going to do that," I just walk away.

That's the best way to approach it, but, of course, I can do this because I am a consultant/vendor, and not an employee. But not everybody has that luxury. If you need the job and can't walk away, then you are placed in a very difficult position. If you continue to push your case, you're setting yourself up for failure, and that will hurt your track record, which is how future employees will evaluate you. Even if you have some successes to point to, if your track record is spotty with significant failures, the employer will be less inclined to take a leap of faith on your word.

There are a lot of companies who get this and want to do things the right way. They are reasonable and they listen. They're the ones you want to work for! Ultimately, you need to be selective and pick your battles. I wouldn't bother trying to convince somebody who wasn't prepared to listen! It sounds arrogant but, if I was looking for a Country Manager job, I would be interviewing the company as much as they are interviewing me!

FRANK: It's often said that what foreigners bring to a Japanese operation is a western approach to strategy and marketing, and that a Japanese national wouldn't have been trained in that way. Is this something you've come across?

SCOTT: It's true they weren't trained in that way, but also the Japanese consumer is not trained in that way either. What motivates Japanese consumers is very different and this is not well understood by new entrants. They will use a bilingual marketing agency, not realizing that they might not be the best choice to reach their target consumers. I was reminded of this just the other day when I was watching Japanese commercials on the in-car screen. I would never have looked at any of these commercials and thought, "Oh yes! That's a good idea!" It's also a reminder of why "two-in-a-box" is the way to go in Japan.

Given these differences, I think patience is very important in this market. Whether it's about deciding the best strategy, or the best marketing agency, or the best Country Manager, you should never put yourself under so much pressure that you're forced into a decision by a deadline. If I was looking for the best marketing campaign, I would want to talk to as many marketing agencies as possible and really make sure that they understand our product. It might take more time, but in Japan, going in when you really know that you have the right foundation, and you are not trying to force it, will always give you a better result.

NOTES and REFERENCES

[1] We contacted contributors initially by email requesting their participation in this project. We provided an overview of the goals of the book and sample topics but encouraged them to speak freely about the issues most important to them. Interviews were conducted over video calls due to Covid. Contributors were offered the option of using a pseudonym.

[2] 深 沼 光(他)増加する外国人経営者とその全像、日本政策金融公庫総合研究所、日本政策金融公庫論集 第51号(2021年 7 月)pp. 8~12 (Fukanuma, Hikaru et. al. 2021. *The Growing Number of Foreign Managers in Japan*. Japan Finance Corporation Research Institute. pp. 8~12.)

[3] "End of the travelling circus: Who needs expats these days?", p.59 in *The Economist*. 18 September 2021

[4] Frank Marton. 4 January 2023. "Sumo, Samurai & Sony: Differentiation as the Key to Success." Speaking on *Japan Expert Insights Clubhouse*.

[5] For a very interesting study into the "insider/outsider" question, see Pandey, Sheela, and Rhee, Shanggeun. 2015. "An Inductive Study of Foreign CEOs of Japanese Firms." Pp. 202-216 in *Journal of Leadership & Organizational Studies*. Vol. 22(2)

[6] For an excellent example of a non-Japanese "Japan-insider" applying a foreign perspective to create positive change, see the work of Adam Fulford in rural Japan including his "Video Bento" project (brief video introduction)
(https://www.youtube.com/watch?v=I-iU0k5mMYw)

[7] Kurimoto, Suguru. 17 November 2020. "Walmart Finds US-Style Retail A Tough Sell In Japan". *Nikkei Asia*
(https://asia.nikkei.com/Business/Business-deals/Walmart-finds-US-style-retail-a-tough-sell-in-Japan)

[8] "Tesco Admits Defeat In Japan", 31 August 2011 in *The Guardian*
(https://www.theguardian.com/business/2011/aug/31/tesco-japan-pull-out-philip-clarke)

[9] "Boots Walks Out On Japan", 14 July 2001 in *The Guardian*
(https://www.theguardian.com/business/2001/jul/14/japan.internationalnews)

[10] Former Boots executive, Noriko Silvester, speaking on "Japan Top Business Interviews, Episode 100, 30 April 2022
(https://www.dale-carnegie.co.jp/en/library/video/top-interviews-100/)

[11] "Hong Kong fund to sell Burger King stakes in South Korea and Japan", 17 January 2022 in *Nikkei Asia* (https://asia.nikkei.com/Business/Food-Beverage/Hong-Kong-fund-to-sell-Burger-King-stakes-in-South-Korea-Japan)

[12] "McDonald's secret sauce for success in Japan". Japan Times Online. 19 September 2017. (https://www.japantimes.co.jp/news/2017/09/19/business/corporate-business/mcdonalds-secret-sauce-success-japan/)

[13] "McDonald's Japan to post highest operating profit of 285m", NikkeiAsia.com, 2 February 2021. (https://asia.nikkei.com/Business/Companies/McDonald-s-Japan-to-post-highest-operating-profit-of-285m)

[14] アマゾン日本事業の売上高は約3.2兆円、ドルベースは243億ドル（前期比5.7%増）【Amazonの2022年実績まとめ】、Impress Business Media、2023年2月8日("Amazon Japan Sales Up 5.7% to 3.2 trillion yen ($24.3 billion), Impress Media, 8 February 2023.)

[15] For example, as on display at an *ukiyoe* exhibition on home delivery in the Edo period at the Ota Memorial Museum of Art in October 2022.

[16] As reported on The Japan Newspapers & Editors Association homepage (www.pressnet.or.jp/english/data/circulation/circulation03.php)

[17] "平成30年度　宅配便取扱実績について"、国土交通省、令和元年10月1日 (Report on the number of items handled by courier services in 2018, Japanese Ministry of Land, Infrastructure, Transport and Tourism.)

[18] "Once More With Feeling: The Story of Ikea's Success In Japan" (https://www.smejapan.com/business-news/story-ikea-japan/)

[19] "Costco Reshapes Wholesale in Japan", *Japan Today* (https://japantoday.com/category/features/executive-impact/costco-reshapes-wholesale-industry)

[20] "Starbucks Japan: Localization Case Study". *Loc N Apps* (https://locnapps14.medium.com/starbucks-japan-localisation-case-study-f58043160f28)

[21] Examples of Adam Fulford's work from YouTube: "Now How", "The 44 Values: Maeve Grapes", "The 44 Values: Hachijojima, a Pacific Paradise That's Part of Tokyo", "Wisdom from Rural Areas may Shine in this Complicated World"

[22] Schaede, Ulrike. 2020. *The Business Reinvention of Japan: How to Make Sense of the New Japan and Why it Matters*. Stanford University Press. pp.25~31

[23] "Over half of Japan companies suffering from labor shortage: survey". KyodoNews.net.
(https://english.kyodonews.net/news/2022/11/fbc-691d031c4-over-half-of-japan-companies-suffering-from-labor-shortage-survey.html)

[24] Ikeda et al. "The Future of the Japanese Long-Term Employment Society: The Consequences of Post-Industrialization and Increase of Unmarried Workers". *Japan Labor Issues*. Vol.6, No.37. March-April 2022.
(https://www.jil.go.jp/english/jli/documents/2022/037-04.pdf)

[25] Definition from Kopp, Rochelle. ""*Monozukuri* - Another Look at a Key Japanese Principle". Japanintercultural.com.
(https://japanintercultural.com/free-resources/articles/*monozukuri*-another-look-at-a-key-japanese-principle/)

[26] Kopp, Rochelle. "Japan's disengaged workers". Japan Intercultural Consulting Website
(https://japanintercultural.com/free-resources/articles/japans-disengaged-workers/)

[27] Shimazu et al. 2010. "Why Japanese workers show low work engagement: An item response theory analysis of the Utrecht Work Engagement scale". *BioPsychoSocial Medicine*
(https://www.ncbi.nlm.nih.gov/pmc/articles/PMC2990723/)

[28] Ikemizu et al. 2022. "Issues in Introduction of Concept of Employee Engagement in Japanese Companies". EPiC *Series in Computing*. Vol. 81, p.395

[29] Abdalla, Almoamen. 26 September 2019. "Japan the Risk Averse". *Nippon.com*
(https://www.nippon.com/en/japan-topics/g00728/japan-the-risk-averse.html)

[30] Online conversation with co author Frank Foley

[31] Kopp, Rochelle. "Overcoming Japanese Risk Adverseness". *Japanintercultural.com*
(https://japanintercultural.com/free-resources/articles/overcoming-japanese-risk-adverseness/)

[32] "Country Rankings: Lawyers Per Capita by Country". 2023. *World Population Review.*
(https://worldpopulationreview.com/country-rankings/lawyers-per-capita-by-country)
"Lawyer Population by State"
https://www.ilawyermarketing.com/lawyer-population-state/
(https://worldpopulationreview.com/country-rankings/lawyers-per-capita-by-country)

[33] Iwata, Mari. ""The Secret to Surviving Japan's Competitive Legal Market?". *Asian Legal Business*. 10 February 2022.
(https://www.ilawyermarketing.com/lawyer-population-state/)

[34] 2022 EF English Proficiency Index ranks Japan as 80th out of 111 countries surveyed. South Korea ranked 36th and China 62nd.

[35] "Japan's Youth Lack Interest in Studying Abroad. That's a Problem for Japanese Businesses" in The Diplomat. 25 June 2021 quotes data from the Japanese Ministry of Education, Culture, Sports, Science, and Technology showing that the number of Japanese students studying abroad peaked at 83,000 in 2004, and has since continued its decline to less than 60,000 per year.
(https://thediplomat.com/2021/06/japans-youth-lack-interest-in-studying-abroad-thats-a-problem-for-japanese-businesses/)

[36] Christensen, Clayton M. et al. 2016. *Competing Against Luck: The Story of Innovation and Customer Choice*. Harper Business.

[37] Hill, Brandon. "The Lies, Myths and Secrets of Japanese UI Design" on *Disrupting Japan: Startups and Innovation in Japan Podcast* 7 March 2023.
(https://www.disruptingjapan.com/the-lies-myths-and-secrets-of-japanese-ui-design/)

[38] Abreu, Rafael. "What is the Studio System in Hollywood?". *Studiobinder.com*. 1 January 2023.
(https://www.studiobinder.com/blog/what-is-the-studio-system-in-hollywood/)

[39] Brueggemann Tom. "A Guide to How Each Studio Now Handles Theatrical Windows". *Indiewire.com*. 22 July 2021.
(https://www.indiewire.com/2021/07/each-hollywood-studio-theatrical-windows-1234652708)

[40] Richards, Rachel. "Hollywood vs Streaming". Worldfinance.com. 2 August 2022.
(https://www.worldfinance.com/special-reports/hollywood-vs-streaming)

[41] Disclosure: At the time of writing, co-author Frank Foley was consulting for The East India Company on their Japan strategy.

[42] ジョエル・サートレイ アーサー・ビナード。2018年。"ずっと　ずっと　かぞく"。ハーパーコリンズ・ジャパン (Original English Version: Sartore, Joel. 2017. "*Animal Ark: Celebrating our Wild World in Poetry and Pictures*". National Geographic Kids.

[43] Definitions from Kopp, Rochelle. "*Monozukuri* — Another Look at a Key Japanese Principle". Japanintercultural.com. (https://japanintercultural.com/free-resources/articles/*monozukuri*-another-look-at-a-key-japanese-principle/)

[44] "The Inside Story". from Hays Japan Website. (https://www.eomelbourne.org/blog/strengthening-your-2ic)

[45] Sullivan, Tim. "*Truth vs Harmony in an American-Japanese Conference Call*". japaninsight.wordpress.com. 27 February 2022. (https://japaninsight.wordpress.com/2020/02/27/truth-versus-harmony-in-an-american-japanese-conference-call/#comments)

[46] "Strengthening Your 2IC as a Way of Strengthening Your Business". *EO Melbourne.org*. 1 March 2022. (https://www.eomelbourne.org/blog/strengthening-your-2ic)

[47] "5 Essential Practices of Great Second-In-Commands". *michaelytimms.com*
(https://michaeltimms.com/5-practices-of-great-2ics/)

[48] Christiansen, Evelyn T and Tanner Pascale, Richard.
"Honda (A)". Harvard Business School, Product #: 384049-PDF-ENG. 23 August 23 1983.
(https://store.hbr.org/product/honda-a/384049); and
"Honda (B)". Product #: 384050-PDF-ENG.
(https://store.hbr.org/product/honda-b/384050?fromSkuRelated=384049&ab=store_idp_relatedpanel_-_honda_b_384050)

[49] https://www.pearsonpte.com/pte-academic

[50] Peter, Laurence J. and Hull, Raymond. 1969. The Peter Principle. William Morrow & Co Inc. (Pan Books ed.)

INDEX

Printed in Japan
落丁、乱丁本のお問い合わせは
Amazon.co.jp カスタマーサービスへ

11542267R00137